# CRICKET
## FUNDAMENTALS

## Peter Philpott

Batsford Ltd, London

Published in association with A H & A W Reed Pty Ltd Sydney

*First published in Great Britain 1982*

Set by ASA Typesetters, Sydney
Printed in Hong Kong
for the publishers
B T Batsford Ltd
4 Fitzhardinge Street
London W1H 0AH

British Library Cataloguing-in-Publication Data
Philpott, Peter
  Cricket fundamentals.
  1. Cricket
  I. Title
796.35'82'024372 GV917
ISBN 0-7134-4456-8

# Contents

# Acknowledgments

Photographs in this book have come from various sources including Central Press Photos Ltd, John Fairfax and Sons Ltd, Milton Wordley, Australian Associated Press and Patrick Eagar. We thank them for their co-operation which has made the excellent collection of photos in this book possible.

The author and publisher have made every effort to contact holders of copyright in this volume. The publisher would be pleased to receive advice of any inadvertent omission.

**Below** *Benaud bowls Peter May around his legs at Old Trafford. This wicket was the beginning of an incredible Australian fight-back and victory.*

**Opposite page** *Richie Benaud, one of the greatest leg-spinners the world has known, delivers a leg-break from a copy-book delivery position.*

# Foreword

Australians have always been inclined to insist their very best cricketers have achieved that status without being coached. There is some kind of inverted snobbery about it, I suppose—that the colonials have made it without all the 'guff' of the country where the game began so long ago. Happily, all that is changing now, with ex-players, coaches and present-day players combining to produce a varied coaching system throughout Australia.

To write a successful coaching book requires more than ability to bat and bowl. A profound knowledge of the game is of paramount importance, but an ability to impart that knowledge is essential.

I've known a lot of cricketers in my time— some great players, some good, some ordinary. I've seen a lot of young cricketers desperately keen to learn and to be coached, but unfortunately their coach has often been unable to instruct or cajole them along the correct lines.

For me, the first thing must always be the fundamentals in coaching. The coach must adhere to them in the same way as he must persuade his charges to attend to the fundamentals of batting, bowling and fielding.

Then, when the youngsters have it right, I like to see them go out and play for the sheer enjoyment of the game. If they are batsmen, to belt the cover off the ball; if bowlers, to try to hit the stumps or take a wicket every ball; if specialist fieldsmen, to do their job with tremendous enthusiasm.

This, combined with those basic fundamentals, cannot fail to produce good cricketers. *Conveying the message is the important thing, and there are few more capable to do that than Peter Philpott.*

I suppose some may say that he begins with an advantage because he is trained as a schoolteacher. Not all schoolteachers are able to transmit their knowledge of an academic subject to their pupils—and, in the same way, not all sporting coaches can get the message across. *But this one can, and does.*

A fine book by a splendid coach and great lover of the game. It is a tremendous pleasure for me to pen a few words to commend the following pages.

RICHIE BENAUD

# Preface

Cricket is still a very healthy game. Over the centuries of its history, many prophets have warned of its decline—but the game has outlived the prophets.

There are always youngsters coming along who are intrigued and drawn to cricket, and there are always adults whose lives are more or less controlled by it.

It is difficult to recognise what attracts us—since cricket, even more than most sports, appears on analysis as a strange and eccentric ritual.

Certainly cricket has been the core of my life for over thirty-five years now, since those days as a young six-year-old when my brothers took me down to the coaching classes at Manly Oval in Sydney. Over that period of time, my own cricket career developed through the grades of club cricket, into Sheffield Shield then Test cricket. It took me to every part of the cricketing world on an indescribable adventure of people and places during twenty years or so.

Then cricket coupled with schoolteaching led to coaching and this has blossomed into a separate career, which looks as if it might be as long and exciting as playing itself.

It has been my pleasure during this time to write widely and often about the game. My enthusiasm has not waned, and I love and respect the old game—and owe a great deal to it. I want youngsters to share my enthusiasm and to enjoy what I have enjoyed, and if this book encourages their 'cricket fever', I shall consider the effort involved fully justified.

*The ground that I shall always regard as my cricketing home—the Sydney Cricket Ground. I believe it is the best player's ground in the world.*

7

# 1 The 'Real' Cricketer

There is more to cricket than being a skilful batsman or bowler. The 'real' cricketer attempts to learn and understand all facets of the game. A batsman is interested in unravelling the mysteries of swing or spin bowling; a bowler is interested in the techniques of wicket-keeping or opening batting; and every player needs to be fully aware of the game in order to 'read developments' whilst fielding.

One simple explanation of this acquisition of all-round knowledge is that a batsman plays better against bowling he understands; a wicket-keeper is lost without a thorough knowledge of spin bowling; and the knowledgeable fieldsman can be relied upon by his captain without constant supervision.

The real cricketer, whether a Test player or

**Opposite**  *There are mysteries about the game of cricket that cannot be explained. The atmosphere of Lord's Cricket Ground, London—still the home of cricket—is just such a mystery. Here Greg Chappell—a 'real' cricketer in every sense—returns to the pavilion after making 131.*

**Below**  *The real cricketer never stops learning and never stops wanting to learn. Experienced Test players Ray Illingworth and John Edrich scrutinise what is going on as they wait to bat at the Sydney Cricket Ground nets.*

a club player, wants to investigate the entire game because he is absorbed completely in its intricacies and atmosphere. Of course he wants to know how to bowl the googly, the off-cutter; of course he wants to know how to play the late cut or sweep shot; or when to give or stop a single. Some of these skills he may never perfect or even use, but he will wish to accumulate this knowledge for the sake of his understanding and enjoyment of the game.

Unfortunately players have even reached 'first-class' cricket without 'knowing' the game. They usually reveal this in their out-cricket. Their captains need to watch them constantly, explaining to them, motioning to them. They are unable—or unwilling—to foresee developments, to study individual batsmen, to anticipate a captain's plan. Consequently they are not contributing as fully as they should to team effort. They may be outstanding batsmen or bowlers, but they are often not as valuable to a team as a slightly less talented player who knows the game thoroughly.

Broadening your understanding of the game is not solely for interest's sake. It also makes you a better cricketer, a player who can fully utilise his ability. Certainly the more you know about the skills and methods of cricket, the more fascinating it becomes. It is such a complex game that all who play it continue to learn forever. Often the learning comes from the most unexpected people and places.

One of the strengths of cricket is the generosity of fellow cricketers. Seldom have I met experienced players who are unwilling to share their knowledge with a youngster. On the contrary most go out of their way to aid all those interested. There is very little age-group jealousy in cricket.

But this generosity creates its own problems. The young player may be bombarded by advice from every side, all well intentioned and some of it useful, some not. The youngster must learn to accept all advice with grace and gratitude, but then to consider it—perhaps discuss it—and eventually *decide for himself* whether it is applicable or not. No one else can make this final decision.

The player who attempts to follow advice from all quarters without due consideration is doomed to a career of frustrating theory; the player who listens to no one will one day realise how much time he has wasted; but the player who listens, considers, balances and then makes *his* decision is the one who will succeed.

The following chapters offer advice, and discuss many techniques and attitudes. You will need to consider these chapters and make your own decisions. The advice given is not aimed only at specialists but also at youngsters, forming part of their cricket education. I hope that all cricketers—young players, old players and non-players—find interest in the following pages.

# SECTION I   BATTING

# 2   Batsman's Check List

1   Be prepared in plenty of time. Don't put yourself in the position where you must rush and become flustered. Make sure clothing and equipment are well adjusted—boots well tied, pads buckled and tucked in correctly; thigh pad and box comfortable and well adjusted; shirt well tucked in; gloves and bat checked. Now settle back and watch the play, preferably in the same light you are to bat in.

2   Don't get ready too early. Don't be one of four padded up and waiting, waiting—for an eternity. Sometimes it will be difficult to avoid such a wait, but do try and have only the next one or two batsmen padded up.

3   Watch the play carefully. What can you learn about the state of the wicket? The opposing bowlers? Fieldsmen? Weather conditions? Then prepare yourself accordingly.

4   If you become uncomfortably nervous, stand up and walk around. Get the blood moving. But never expect to overcome the nerves totally. Most of us have butterflies and, under control, they may do some good.

5   A wicket has fallen—it is your turn to go in. Get out there before the out-going man has left the field of play. Don't stand chatting to him. Move out briskly, but take time to accustom your eyes to the light.

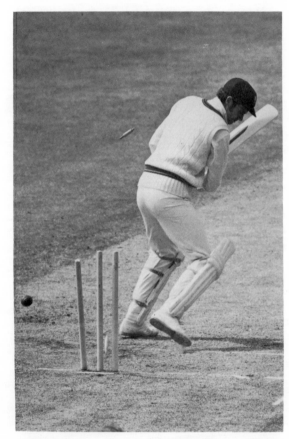

*'Eventually, inevitably, you are going to get out.' It happens to the greatest players, such as Greg Chappell who was clean bowled by Grahame Roope.*

6 Don't spend an eternity discussing conditions and tactics with the not-out batsman. Once you are out there, get on with it as soon as possible.

7 Take guard! Check what is said in later pages—what guard is most suited to your stance? Don't take 'centre' just because 'everyone else does'. Mark the guard carefully with spikes or bat, then recheck it.

8 Check the field placement. Where are the gaps for early singles to get you off the mark and bring your more settled partner to the batting end?

9 Now prepare yourself to face the bowler and concentrate. Remember your first role is to play yourself in, to build an innings. This will be done best by playing straight and settling down before attempting to play too many shots. 'Playing straight' means preferring the shots played with a vertical bat rather than the horizontal. On the other hand, try not to get bogged down. This will only allow bowlers a psychological advantage. Pick up your singles, playing a support role for your partner at first, but also hit any bad balls—short or full—hard towards the gaps. Memorise those major gaps that coincide with your strong shots. As you build your

*Sometimes when chasing runs, you may have to sacrifice your wicket for the team. Ross Edwards sacrificed his wicket in the Prudential Cup Championship against the West Indies at the Oval.*

innings try to assess the wicket, weather, bowling and fielding. Begin to plan your innings. Certain factors will affect your plan:

**The state of the wicket**   If it is hard, true and fast, you will limit your errors if you play forward when in doubt. This means go back to the shortball, forward to the full. If you are uncertain, a decision to play back on a fast wicket could be your final decision, so go forward when in doubt. The only type of bowler who can force an adjustment to this plan in these conditions is the real speedster.

If the wicket is slow so that the ball is not coming onto you, reverse the procedure and go back when in doubt. A wicket of this type could be caused by dampness or by over-dryness; occasionally, too, the ball may dig in and kick. On the back foot you are in a better position to deal with this. *Remember that most wet wickets are easy to bat on if you adjust your technique.* Many bowlers bowl too short on wet wickets, and if you are looking for the back foot, you have all the time in the world to pull and cut.

If the wicket is consistently keeping low, you must favour the front foot. Only go back when you have to and try not to play across the ball.

If the wicket is erratic in bounce and pace, there is not much advice I can give you. You will have to play it by instinct and do the best you can. If the bowlers are not using these conditions well, you may gain an advantage. If they are bowling well, you will have to choose whether to try and sit it out or whether to hit your way out of it. If the field is up around the bat, lofting may well be the safer alternative.

**Different types of bowlers**   When facing the real speedster or a seamer who is swinging abnormally, you may find an initial back-foot commitment advan-

tageous. The back foot begins to move back and towards off-stump as the ball is delivered. If it is short of a length—which it will be with most speedsters—you continue into a back-foot position. If the delivery proves to be well up, however, the front foot moves forward again and you play 'half-cocked'. This technique gives you surprisingly more time to see the ball. It may limit your scope for front-foot driving, but will help you settle down. It may well be only used as a temporary tactic until you develop your attack.

Against all other types on good wickets you are safer on the front foot whilst you

*A wicket has fallen—move out briskly, just as Ian Chappell did at the Adelaide Oval.*

settle down. This certainly does not mean chasing a spinner metres down the wicket at this stage. Simply have a look at the bowler on the front foot from the crease as you build your innings. Eventually, though, you must develop your attack. As each bowler offers his wares, you begin to calculate his weaknesses and strengths. Is there a greater chance to get at him by going down the wicket? This may mean missing out on the occasional ball a little short of a length, but you cannot have it all ways. Check the major field-placement gaps and go down after him.

For some bowlers you may well decide the opportunities are greater on the back foot. Now you look for the back-foot movement to utilise hook, pull, cut or back-foot drive. In so doing you may miss out on the occasional front-foot drive. But you are trying to develop a plan that will allow you to attack each bowler. Perhaps you may need to readjust your plan as the game goes on. Certainly this is what the experienced bowler will be doing to try and counter your plan.

Clearly you must have attacking shots off both front and back foot. Preferably you want shots in both positions that you know you can hit for four with some regularity. You don't need all the shots, but you must have your drilled boundary shots which you can control and place.

**The position of the game**   Nine times out of ten when a batsman comes to the crease, it is to the advantage of his team to play his natural game. In other words, by playing for himself the batsman is playing for his team. The more runs you can score, the better it is for your team as a whole.

The very slow, shotless player can be an exception. If he bats on and on, occupying the crease without scoring, the bowlers get on top, the batting team's morale falls and, later, wickets will probably have to be sacrificed to make up for his slowness.

Under normal circumstances, this player is better out than shutting the game up once he has settled down.

There is an occasional game in which victory becomes impossible, and a team fights for a draw. More often the situation occurs when a gamble, some fast running between wickets and calculated hitting, can turn a potential draw into a thrilling victory. Now all members of the team must respond and forget themselves.

10 So you build your innings and your plan of attack. First you support your partner who has been in longer; when he gets out you become the senior partner who must take over the scoring responsibility and support your new partner as he settles down.

11 At times it may be necessary to pull your concentration together; perhaps you may tire. Take block again and start again. It may help to break your score into tens. Score ten, tick it off and then begin another ten.

12 As we said, you may need to adjust your approach according to the position of the game. You may increase or decrease run rates, protect or play a secondary role to a partner. Try to do what is best for the team.

13 Eventually, inevitably, you are going to get out. When it happens, take it well, take it sportingly. If the finger is up, there's nothing you can do about it, so get off the field briskly without a temperamental performance. You must make your decision about 'walking'—that is, leaving the wicket automatically if you know you are out.

14 When you get back to your team-mates, don't make them suffer your bad temper. You may be disappointed, but be man enough to accept it and not sulk or grizzle. Your team-mates are usually sympathetic.

15 Finally, think over your innings and dismissal carefully. Where did you make errors? What good things did you do?

'*So get off the field briskly without a temperamental performance.*' *Garfield Sobers sets a good example here at the Melbourne Cricket Ground.*

## Batsman's Check List

What did you learn about wickets, conditions, bowlers, fieldsmen? Was there anything that baffled you? From every innings you should learn something. From every mistake you should learn something. What you learn is stored away and can be recalled when necessary. You won't wish to repeat the same mistake. Between matches learn what you can about the art of bowling. Start by reading what this book has to say.

Batting is an art. In few games do eleven players concentrate on defeating one player. In few games are you allowed only one chance. It is difficult, it can be frustrating, but success makes all the hard work worthwhile.

*'When it happens, take it well, take it sportingly', as South African champion, Graham Pollock, did at the Mebourne Cricket Ground.*

# 3 Basics of Batsmanship

Batting should be based on attack. Take a positive attitude that you defend only when you cannot attack, rather than a negative attitude of defending first and attacking if possible. Of course this does not mean hitting the cover off every ball, but do emphasise attack in your matches and practices. Particularly you should develop attacking shots off both the front and the back foot.

Naturally any good player will build an innings. Allow yourself time to settle down at the crease before unleashing all your shots. This certainly does not mean shotless defence for the first twenty minutes; full tosses or long hops should be hit hard at any time. Early in your innings treat each ball on its merits, play straight and gauge the pace, bounce, spin of the wicket, as well as the quality of bowling and fielding. At this stage limit your risks, don't try to make a bad ball out of a good ball, but settle down and have a look.

Even so, to remain scoreless during this period allows fielding teams to get on top, and puts you and your team at a psychological disadvantage. So look for singles, and hit the bad ball hard. This way the score keeps on mounting, batsmen keep on changing ends and a bowler's attack is disrupted; the batting side does not become despondent.

When great players build their innings you are hardly aware that they are scoring early. It comes as a shock when you look at the scoreboard to find them with forty-odd runs to their credit. You realise that they are just settling down and have not yet unfolded their shots or really begun to attack you. Norm O'Neill at his top was a perfect example of this. After half an hour of batting he was twenty or thirty from singles and controlled strokes, but with no really memorable shot. And then gradually he unleashed and ... bang! No one who saw them will ever forget those two centuries he made against Victoria in 1957.

Each batsman realises his limitations and develops his game accordingly. He learns that he has certain weak shots and perhaps eliminates them from his repertoire. But it is dangerous to do this when you are young and without sound advice. Rather than looking for weaknesses, look for strengths; rather than eliminating weak shots, practise and correct them to make them strengths also. Think positively.

The teacher, coach or manager should be helping youngsters to develop their individual attacking games as well as helping team performances. To stifle youthful aggression for the sake of 'a big gold cup' at this stage is unforgivable. So if a youngster has very sound defence but lacks shots, aggression must be emphasised at his practices rather than an attempt be made to create an impregnable fortress.

When I first saw Doug Walters in the nets, I was critical of his batting. His defence appeared brittle as he attempted to hit everything with power off his back foot through mid-wicket or the covers. But Doug was intending to develop his back-foot power. He or an adviser—who may well have been Richie Benaud—had realised that to reach the top as a first-class batsman you must be able to score heavily off the back foot as well as the front. Dependence on front-foot drives plus front-foot defence may get you through in club cricket, but in the first-class game you must have strong run-scoring shots off the back foot.

Doug Walters was *using his batting practice sensibly. He was using it to overcome weaknesses rather than to practise strengths.* I would suggest that if you lack power you use much of your net practices to develop

**Top left**   *One of the world's most dangerous players, Ian Botham on his day can take any attack apart. Here he does so in his great Leeds innings in 1981.*

**Top right**   *Doug Walters learnt early the value of attacking off the back foot. He practised hitting through his back defensive shots, as we see him do here at the Western Australian Cricket Association nets.*

**Bottom left**   *Check Doug Walters' stance with the requirements given in this chapter. Note he chooses to place the bat behind his right toe.*

attacking shots. If you cannot do this in the nets, where can you do it?

I have no doubt that in the long run, aggression is vital to batting success. Certainly the saying that 'attack is the best form of defence' is appropriate. For the future of cricket, this is the way the game must be played.

Many players and spectators who recall some of my own innings may guffaw at this emphasis on aggression. On far too many occasions I allowed defence to dominate my game. I recognise this error and realise that too early in my career I began to adapt to limitations instead of overcoming them. I lacked powerful back-foot shots and often made it too easy for some bowlers to bog me down.

Combined with aggression must be concentration and determination. No amount of natural ability can compensate for a lack of these two factors which are closely connected. If you lack these powers, or the wish to develop them, then your future in cricket as a whole, not only in batting, is very limited indeed.

But let's assume that you are prepared to concentrate hard, you have determination, fair natural ability and a sensibly aggressive attitude towards batting. What next?

Let's examine the basics of grip, stance and backlift. Then we shall look at all the shots of the game, discuss the major errors and how to correct them.

## GRIP, STANCE AND TAKING BLOCK

The most common error amongst young batsmen is to hold the bat with hands apart. A coach never wants to stifle individuality, but few batsmen have succeeded with hands apart. For 99 per cent of us, 'hands togetherness' is essential. In golf the two hands overlap to ensure co-operation; but in cricket we ask only that they stay together.

This error usually develops when a youngster, picking up dad's or big brother's bat, can only balance the enormous implement by stretching his hands wide apart. So make sure your bat is small enough and light enough to manoeuvre with hands together.

And why together? Because the two hands must work in harmony for best results. Normally the bottom hand on the bat is physically the stronger, and separated from its partner it will tend to take over too much of the work with sad results. This 'bottom handedness' is a very common batting fault which is discussed later.

If hands are together at the top of the handle, control of the bat can be difficult. If they are at the bottom of the handle, or 'choking the splice', power may be lost with front-foot shots and 'bottom handedness' be encouraged. So let's have hands together towards the middle of the handle. Fingers and thumbs of both hands should be right around the handle. Don't allow a thumb or first finger to run down behind handle or blade.

Now check the grip of both hands. Lie the bat face down and grasp the handle with your top hand in a 'shake hands' grip. You will notice now that the V created by the first finger and thumb of this hand is about halfway between the splice and the outside edge of the bat. The bottom hand now grips the bat so that its V, of the first finger and thumb, is immediately below that of the top hand. The top hand grips so that the back of this hand faces towards mid-off or cover. This hand should not be behind the handle with the knuckles facing you as this can restrict follow through with front-foot shots. Check the position of this top hand by extending the first finger, which should be about parallel to the bottom forearm.

Youngsters should be encouraged to retain this grip unchanged for all shots in their formulative years, for there is no real reason to slip the top hand behind the handle for defensive shots.

So we are gripping the bat correctly. What now?

The general stance must be comfortable. Most players stand comfortably with feet

slightly apart (about 15 centimetres), knees slightly bent and both feet parallel to the batting crease. Weight is evenly balanced on both feet. To lean heavily on the front foot anchors it and telegraphs an intention to play back; whilst back-foot leaning indicates forward play. We want to be able to play back or forward with equal ease, so let's be evenly balanced on both feet.

Just as bowling is a side-on art, so is batting. The batsman eyes the bowler along the line of the front shoulder with head up and eyes level. Don't crouch too much, since you'll have to unbend before playing a shot. Don't bob up and down as this will be moving the level of your eyes. An imaginary line joining the toes of both feet should lead to the bowler. Remember to adjust the position of your feet to the position of the bowler's delivery. You cannot expect to stand in the same position against a right hand over the wicket as against a right hand round the wicket bowler.

*This Victorian batsman facing John Snow at the Melbourne Cricket Ground has picked the bat up early and reasonably straight. Note that he has made an initial commitment back and across towards off-stump against the pace of Snow.*

Many youngsters, however, exaggerate their side-on stance and come too far around, almost presenting their back-side to the bowler. They are creating a blind spot for themselves on and outside the leg-stump for, with this stance, bowlers are virtually bowling behind the batsman.

On the other hand, many older players square-up and become more chest-on to the bowler. I am guilty of this and some say this is because your neck loses flexibility in old age—but there are other reasons. Two-shouldered or chest-on players are looking for on-side play, and are usually prepared to do the extra work necessary to compensate for their off-side vulnerability. Most of these players are experienced, know the orthodox method, understand the advantages and disadvantages of what they are doing, but have decided that it suits them as individuals.

It is unwise for youngsters to copy such stances until they too become experienced and have experimented with the orthodox way. Otherwise they could be creating problems for themselves which they do not understand and cannot counter.

With our stance settled and the bat gripped correctly, we now have to place the bottom of the bat down somewhere. Many players place their bat next to the little toe of the back foot, or fully behind the back foot. Successful players have used many different positions, so I won't argue as long as you're comfortable. But what does interest me is that where you place that bat will determine whether your stance is 'wide open' or 'closed'. In turn, this will determine the block (or 'centre') you take before facing up to the bowler.

To complete your stance now, simply pull in the handle to rest naturally on the front thigh. You should now be in a comfortable position awaiting the bowler to deliver the ball.

Many youngsters begin their innings with the ceremony of taking 'centre' without understanding what they are doing. A guard, or block, is taken to give a batsman the assurance that his legs are outside the line of the leg-stump. Now he can confidently play shots off his legs with the knowledge that—by the rules anyway—he cannot be out leg before wicket (check your rules!).

But taking 'centre' does not necessarily give this assurance. If you have a very closed stance with bat tucked behind the feet, this guard will leave your legs in line with leg-stump. I remember having to suffer for this error as a boy. Playing off my legs and missing, I was frequently, to my amazement, given out leg before wicket. No one explained to me that with my closed stance I was indeed standing with legs very close to the line of the leg-stump.

If you have a closed stance, you must take 'leg-stump' guard, or as it is often called 'one leg'. A semi-closed stance with bat tapping back toe requires a 'centre and leg' ('two leg') guard to ensure safety. Only the wide open stance with bat well away from the feet can confidently take 'centre'. Most first-class players take a 'two leg' guard; but don't be an imitator, work your guard out according to the requirements of your stance.

## PICKING UP THE BAT

So we are all set to begin batting, with our stance and grip settled and with our feet correctly positioned. What now?

Well, now comes the beginning of difficulties as we enter into competition with eleven players, each one of whom wants to get rid of us batsmen as quickly as possible. Batting is a very difficult art which requires a great deal of thought, concentration, determination and *practice*.

It may sound elementary to state that before we can play any shot, we must first raise the bat—but this is where many batsmen begin to create problems for themselves. First, some pick the bat up too late after the ball has been delivered instead of that instant prior to delivery. Most of these players are late in their eventual foot movements. Secondly, others pick up the bat too high early in their innings and create problems against pace bowling or against any bowling on faster wickets. As you begin to build your innings limit the backlift to avoid errors, and as the innings develops lift higher to allow greater power.

But the most common error is to pick up entirely with the bottom hand. The top hand should be lifting whilst the bottom hand balances, otherwise there is the tendency to bring the bat down across the line of flight. I am not insisting that backlift must be 'straight' (that is, picked up over the stumps rather than towards slips), although with practice, if it is comfortable, to do so is probably advantageous. But certainly when the bat does not come down straight, you are creating problems for yourself.

*Too much bottom hand has dragged the face of the bat across the ball in this shot.*

*Intikhab Alam suffers the fate of all batsmen who continue 'to hit across the ball'.*

This is all part of the strong bottom hand problem I mentioned earlier. When the bottom hand controls pick-up, it will tend to dominate all phases of batting. And what happens then?

Experiment for yourself by holding the bat in a clenched bottom fist only. You will notice that your pick-up is now naturally towards third slip, whilst, as you bring the bat down, the face will incline towards the on-side. *The harder you club with that strong bottom hand, the more this inclination 'across' the ball will become. When you hear of a player hitting 'across the line of flight', he is almost certainly clubbing with bottom hand.*

The result is that he does not get the full, open face of the blade onto his off-side shots in particular; he loses timing and frequently finds off-side drives ending up straight or towards mid-on. And the harder he tries to hit the ball at this stage, the worse his timing becomes. You notice the problem most when you are a little out of form, or when you are playing front-foot and off-side shots on slowish wickets.

To overcome this problem is simple. Just understand that your top hand must control pick-up and at least do half the work in leading the face of the blade onto the ball.

Try this method. Do some batting without a bat and imagine that the back of your top hand is the face of the bat. Pick up the imaginary bat and flow into your drives so that you are striking the imaginary bat face cleanly and fully onto the ball in the direction you wish to hit it. Practise this several times, then practise with a real bat and only the top hand (put your other hand behind your back!). Now do the same with top hand as control, and only the thumb and forefinger of the bottom hand holding the handle. Finally allow the entire bottom hand to grasp the handle, but lightly, with the top hand as master. Bear in mind that picture of the back of the top hand being the face of the bat. You should now have the required pick-up and swing.

Many great players have batted successfully with too much bottom hand, but they would admit the advantages of the top hand leading. Certainly if you are an average player, you must be prepared to work on the correct swing, which entails two hands working together and top hand leading. If a golfer needs to perfect one swing, why shouldn't a batsman—who must have half a dozen different swings for different shots, and against a moving ball—practise hard to improve?

# 4 Batting Footwork

Footwork is the basis of batting. Quick feet ensure that eye, body and bat arrive in the right place at the right time. One of the problems for the youngster is to accept the fact that he must move his feet for every shot. The stance is purely an introductory position and no shot should be played from there. Reducing it to simplicity, feet movements are twofold—first there is the movement forward or back, and secondly, but concurrently, a sideways movement towards the ball.

### FORWARD OR BACK?

Basically if the ball is well up, you should play forward. In this way you can strike it on the full or half volley before it is able to deviate as it bounces. On the other hand, if the ball is shorter, the batsman plays back as far as he can within his crease to give himself more room and time to see the ball and make a shot.

Of course such a decision about length—of whether it is over-pitched or short—is an instantaneous one. The major difference between average, good and outstanding bats-

*Two players make the correct decision to defend on the front foot. One is Doug Walters at the Sydney Cricket Ground nets; the other is an unidentified young lady indoors. Both have made their decision on length, and the shots are technically perfect in performance.*

men is this ability to 'see the ball quickly' and to judge length accurately. After all, a fast delivery takes much less than one second to travel the twenty metres between bowler and batsman.

But no matter who the player is, he will at times be undecided whether to play back or forward, or he will make an error. The error will come from a loss of concentration or a bowler's skill in changing his pace or flight. Indecision on whether to play forward or back occurs when the ball is bowled on a good length, that is neither short nor over-pitched. To a good length ball, most players reveal whether they are essentially front- or back-foot players, for most of us have a preference. When in doubt the 'front-foot players' will come forward, and vice versa.

The terms 'front-foot player' and 'back-foot player', however, confuse many youngsters. They mistakenly believe that batsmen always play forward or always play back. This is not so—a skilled batsman must be adept both back and forward, although he probably has greater strength in one or the other.

Of course different types of wickets can alter this preference. A hard, true and fast wicket may favour front-foot play, whilst a dampish one favours back-foot play. On the former you play back only when you must; on the latter you play forward only when you must. But whatever the wicket, batting always entails either back or forward movement against every ball bowled.

## SIDEWAYS MOVEMENT

All defensive and most attacking shots are played with a vertical bat. It limits errors of judgement regarding variations in height, as you have the full length of blade to deal with these variations. However, this vertical (or 'straight') bat now gives you only the width of the blade, less than twelve centimetres, to deal with lateral variations—that is, sideways movement in the air, through spin or cut.

In order to limit errors, the batsman needs to get bat, ball and eyes in one straight line.

To do so when playing forward, he must have his front foot as close to the ball as possible. This is because in a forward position with front knee bent, his eye is above the front foot. On the other hand, with back shots his eye is above the back foot. Thus a forward shot must be both a movement up the pitch and towards the ball, whilst a back shot is not only towards the stumps but also across towards the flight of the ball. In this way you are doing your best to line up bat, ball and eyes to deal best with sideways variations of the ball.

So there is your introductory footwork. With every ball bowled you must decide whether to play back or forward according to its length. When you make this decision, move your body and eyes towards the line of the ball.

One warning! Don't fall into the error of making decisions before the ball is bowled; you can only play according to length. In particular, try not to commit your front foot forward, as an intelligent bowler will see this quickly, shorten his length and make it most difficult to score off your favourite front foot.

Many opening batsmen (amongst them Geoff Boycott) tend to commit themselves onto the back foot before delivery. This is because it gives them a little more time, coupled with the fact that most modern fast bowlers tend to bowl short of a length. In first-class cricket this may well be a worthwhile tactic, but youngsters at this stage should keep their feet still until delivery, then make a decision according to length whether to play back or forward. Whatever happens, avoid itching forward.

## SIDE-ON BATTING

A time-worn coaching instruction that has caused more trouble than it is worth is 'Get behind the ball!'. It is thrown at youngsters right, left and centre and is nearly always misunderstood by player and coach alike. Although the player needs to get *his eyes behind the ball* and vertical bat, he needs to position *his body beside the ball.*

Mike Denness has moved back to Max Walker. Note all the requirements of side-on batting and check the position of back foot and front shoulder. But what is wrong with the hands?

The penalty for neither moving back nor forward, but playing from the crease. Verkat plays from the crease and is bowled for three by Willis.

Ian Davis plays back, chest-on, and gets into an impossible position. Note how the position of his feet and body force the bat to come down across the ball.

Great players such as O'Neill, Miller and Dexter could hit powerfully from a back-foot defensive position. John Parker of New Zealand displays the shot to perfection at the Melbourne Cricket Ground.

25

**Above**  *These two photographs show batsmen in dangerous positions to bumpers for different reasons. First, Ian Chappell has squared-up to John Snow; secondly, Indian opener, Mankad, has ducked head forward and taken his eyes off the ball.*

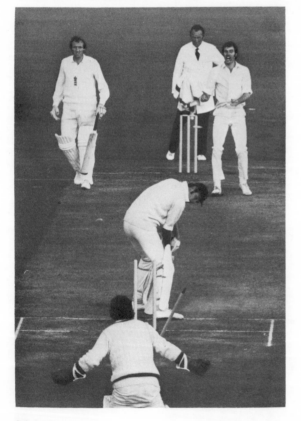

*Tony Greig adopts the straddled defence position against Greg Chappell, but somehow the ball gets through.*

A youngster tends to follow the 'get behind it' instruction verbatim. He plants himself squarely in front of the stumps, toes pointing towards the bowler, with bat straight in front of him. He is now completely chest-on to the bowler in what we call a 'French cricket' stance. In this position, it is only possible to bring the bat down from the original backlift position across the line of the ball. Try it out! *It is impossible to bring the bat down full-faced and straight onto the ball because your body is in the way.*

But there is an even greater problem for the youngster who develops this chest-on defensive position as a habit. An automatic movement into this position when playing back will rob him of many off-side attacking back-foot shots. He will be able to pull, but to force the ball off the back foot with vertical bat through the mid-off to cover-point arc is physically impossible, and cutting is more difficult. Any medium-pace bowler detecting such a batting weakness could restrict scoring completely by bowling a little short of a length on the line of the off-stump.

So don't get behind the ball! Get your eye behind it but your body beside it. Let's examine this method.

When playing back, your back foot moves as far back as possible and towards the line of the ball; your front foot follows back to keep you on balance. But your body stays relatively side-on to the bowler with toes pointing towards point or cover *not* straight back at the bowler. In this position your eyes, the bat and ball are in line and, because your body is not in the way behind the ball, the bat can flow through full-faced and free from the backlift. As well, the batsman is in a perfect position to hit and follow through the defensive shot, turning back defence into powerful back-foot off-side shots. Norm O'Neill, Keith· Miller and Ted Dexter were copy-book examples of this, and none of them could have executed these destructive shots had they been chest-on.

Some very experienced players revert to square-on defence when they are in real trouble. With pads straddled on either side of the bat, they present a wider defensive wall. But to do this they are restricting themselves to defence alone, and certainly indicate their uncertainty of the bowler.

Such a technique, however, is not for youngsters who need the basic footwork that puts them into position to hit powerfully off the back foot, or if they must, to use back defence. And to do this, they must square-up but attempt to stay side-on beside the line of the delivery. So when coaching youngsters, please beware of that catch-cry 'Get behind the ball!'.

Finally, this side-on back foot position is the answer to playing bumpers. From this position the batsman is able to sway inside or outside the line of the rising ball without taking his eye off it, and using his bent back leg as a pivot. The chest-on player, on the other hand, presents a much larger target to the fast bowler's bouncer. Worse still, it is difficult from here to sway inside and outside the ball, the legs become locked, and all too often the only evasive method becomes a forward duck of the head. A head-down duck obviously means losing sight of the ball and is of course physically dangerous.

Many of our first-class batsmen are experiencing this very problem with bouncers. They are getting into this critical squared-up, chest-on, back-foot position—and when fast bouncers arrive they are in real trouble.

# 5  Front-foot Shots

Let's look at those shots played off the front foot to over-pitched deliveries that arrive either on the half volley or low full toss.

You settle into your normal stance, keeping the feet still until the ball is delivered, and you make your decision on its length. If your judgement is that the ball is over-pitched, the movement of your front foot is immediately forward *and towards the pitch of the ball.* As the front leg is moved forward, the knee must be bent to keep body, shoulder and head down.

If the knee is straight, the shoulder and head go up and the ball is lofted. One of the most common faults is to take a short step forward on the front foot with the leg unbent. As you swing, you become unbalanced and the back leg is forced to step forward to regain balance. This limits your reach forward, and you cannot obtain the full body swing that gives fluency and power to all drives. If the front knee is bent and your front leg thrown well forward, you should be perfectly balanced so that your body and leg positions remain constant during the swing and follow through. A sound aim is to try and stay low whilst driving.

The player who 'itches' forward before the bowler bowls creates a problem for himself when driving. In anticipation, his front foot moves straight forward rather than towards the ball. Then if the delivery happens to be wide of off-stump, his foot (and therefore his eyes) is too far from the line of the ball. On the other hand if the ball is on the line of, or outside, leg-stump he finds his leg in the way between bat and ball. He will find it difficult to get around his leg to play a shot, or, if he does play the shot by playing 'behind himself', he is leaving himself open to leg-side snicks. An experienced bowler will quickly recognise such a weakness and concentrate on it.

As we have seen, the secret is to have the full face of the bat coming through in the direction you wish to hit the ball. This is achieved if the front shoulder, with the front foot, leads into the ball. The foot takes the eye into position and the shoulder moves the up-lifted bat into position. Thus, for an off-drive, the movement of the front shoulder towards mid-off forces the uplifted bat towards fine leg. For the on-drive, the front shoulder leading towards mid-on forces the backlift towards slips. For the cover-drive the backlift is moved back between square-leg and leg.

To complete the drive simply requires a full-faced straight swing controlled by the top hand. The bat will flow through straight for each drive to present the full blade, and every swing will be identical once the shoulder has led towards the ball.

When the front shoulder leads straight down the wicket—as so often happens—each swing will be different. Only the straight drive will be a straight swing.

For the off-drive the swing will begin straight then circle outwards in a *hook*. Both swings are wide open to error.

So the basics are clear! Lead with the front shoulder plus front foot and flow through with the top hand. New Zealand's Glenn Turner illustrates this fact perfectly in the picture opposite.

Brian Booth hit the ball with tremendous power but with little effort. He was a perfect example of full-faced timing as opposed to brute strength.

For the on-drive, the swing of the bat is from slips towards mid-on; for the straight drive, from the wicket-keeper towards straight hit; for the off-drive, from fine leg towards mid-off; for the cover-drive, from a

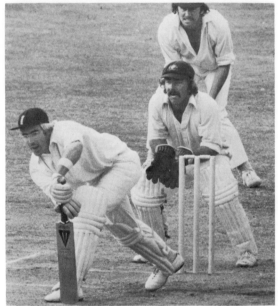

**Top left** *New Zealand's Glenn Turner plays forward with technical perfection. Note the pick-up, the position of front toe, knee and leg; the position of elbow, shoulder and head. The leading of front foot and front shoulder towards the ball is a lesson for everyone.*

**Top right** *Paul Sheehan plays forward defensively with technical perfection, except he has lifted his back foot.*

**Centre right** *David Steele, having pushed straight forward before determining the line of the delivery, is forced to play 'behind himself'. His eyes are not in line with the bat, and any inside edge could offer a leg-side chance.*

**Bottom right** *Dayle Hadlee of New Zealand sets himself for forward defence and does not follow the ball. Although beaten by turn, he remains not out.*

29

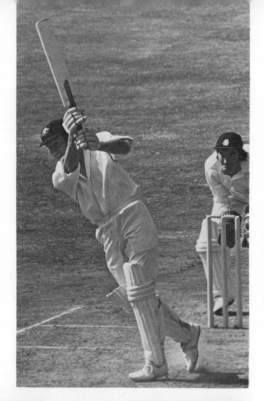

**Top left**   *Ian Chappell leaves his crease and gets down the pitch to drive against England at the Oval.*

**Bottom left**   *The off-drive and cover-drive are amongst the most majestic shots in the game. Note the similarities and differences in the shots played here by Ian Redpath.*

**Top right**   *Viv Richards of the West Indies.*

**Bottom right**   *Dennis Amiss of England.*

wider fine leg towards cover. Unless these adjustments to swing are made, it is impossible to play all these shots with the full face of a vertical bat.

The achievement of the free flow, full-face and vertical bat when driving is based on several factors:

1 The top hand controls the flow of the face of the bat onto the ball. (Think of the back of your top hand as the face of the bat.) Too strong a bottom hand will drag the face of the bat across the ball.

2 Try to point your front shoulder at the pitch of the ball. This will bring you into the side-on position necessary for off-side shots. (When you cover-drive, you half-turn your back on the bowler.)

3 Bend the front knee, try to stay low and, as far as possible, point front foot towards where you are hitting.

4 The elbow of the back arm stays tucked closer in to the body than the front elbow.

5 Watch the ball right onto the bat, then follow the swing through full and free over the front shoulder.

The foot needs to get close to the pitch of the ball so as to get your eyes in line. The wider outside off-stump, the further across goes the front foot. When the ball is on leg-stump, put your foot outside the ball. This gets the leg out of the way, opens up your body for the shot and leaves a pad outside the bat to eliminate the danger of leg-side snicks. Too many youngsters try to on-drive with front leg inside the line of the ball and find themselves trying to play 'around their legs'.

Practise your driving with a friend throwing a ball from 5 to 10 metres onto a marked spot. Use a soft ball indoors. A coach can stand on the off-side of the batsman, drop a tennis ball from head height and ask him to drive it on its second bounce.

In particular look for opportunities to practise your on-driving through mid-wicket. Instead of turning 'around the corner' try to force with the full face through the arc between square-leg and mid-on, usually the biggest gap on the field. Most top batsmen are great on-drivers who consistently time the ball through the on-side field.

## GOING DOWN THE WICKET TO DRIVE

Most Australian batsmen, when settled in, prefer to leave their crease and go down the wicket to drive slow bowlers. In this way, they give a slow bowler little margin for error, and are able to drive safely what was otherwise a good length ball. Bob Simpson and Neil Harvey were so fleet-footed to slows that it was often impossible to hit the ground.

The footwork when going down the wicket is aimed at transferring your driving position two paces further down the wicket. Thus *the body stays side-on with the front shoulder pointing at the ball.* The front foot moves into normal driving position, the back foot comes up and crosses behind the front, then the front foot moves forward again into the driving position. It is important to glide smoothly rather than jump down the wicket so as to avoid moving the eye level. You must move quickly, like lightning, and on the toes. Unless you are very quick, and unless you are certain you can get to the ball on the full or half volley, you should not go down at all. Speedy footwork creates a great challenge for a bowler; but slow movers coming down the wicket are 'money for jam'.

It is quite pointless to walk or run forward chest-on to the bowler, as in this position you cannot drive and to leave your crease with any other initial aim than attack is creating unnecessary risks. Under Australian conditions, no batsman is complete without this speedy footwork and he should work hard to master the technique. Practise the foot movements and perhaps use squash as an exercise to speed up the feet. It is disappointing to see more and more of our younger batsmen adopting the English 'from-the-crease' technique which was developed in conditions quite different from our own.

31

Of course early in your innings you will play from the crease. Limit your risks as you settle in, countering the bowler by playing full stretch forward or well back towards the stumps. Then as you see the ball better, gain confidence and get to know the bowler, you can begin to get down at his fuller deliveries. But whatever happens, don't 'lose your cool' and chase him haphazardly. If you need to go more than two paces, you should be back anyway to what is in fact a short-pitched ball. Many very slow bowlers tend to come off the wicket slowly. If you stay back, you can safely blast several balls an over; but if you chase them, their drop, turn and bounce can get you into real trouble. So retain your discretion and concentration.

Of course to go down you follow normal driving technique by moving not only forward but towards the ball. It is suicide to chase leg-spinners straight down the wicket, as they will widen on you and leave you stranded. Equally disastrous is leaving your crease to deliveries bowled wide of leg-stump, for now you are playing 'behind yourself' and must eventually miss, allowing the leg-spin to curl back to the keeper for the easiest of stumpings.

Instead of going down to this delivery, look for the sweep shot which is always played with back foot anchored and is more destructive.

## THE SWEEP SHOT

The sweep is best played with the front leg at full stretch and bent back knee on the ground. The cross bat swing picks up the ball on the half volley in front of the eyes to dispatch it forward or backward of square-leg, whilst the wrists roll the bat over the ball to keep it on the ground. A talented sweeper can place the ball accurately, hitting it slightly earlier for square shots and delaying it for finer shots. The latter, sweetly slipped towards fine leg, is most difficult to place a field to. Colin Cowdrey and Basil Butcher played this with a peculiar vertical bat method, whilst Peter Burge and Rohan Kanhai were more

orthodox—but any good sweeper makes straying towards the leg-stump very expensive for a spinner.

Against the leg-spinner, make sure your front leg is thrown wider outside leg-stump to cover the break back and the danger of being bowled around the legs. To the off-spinner, however, the front leg can be straight forward, and the shot played with the spin off the line of the stumps. On real turners, many batsmen are prepared to sweep rather than drive off-spinners from any position, even outside off-stump.

Many New Zealanders in particular employ this technique on many of their slow, low wickets; and the English often hit their way out of trouble in this way. But once again, this is post-graduate cricket and youngsters should look for the sweep only against good length or fuller deliveries pitched outside leg-stump.

## THE LOFTED DRIVES

Other effective front-foot attacking shots are the lofted drives. Intelligent lofted driving, as opposed to wild swinging, is difficult to bowl against or place a field to, yet it is quite simple for an established batsman to introduce.

Once again it is essential to use full-faced timing rather than strength and to hit straight between mid-on and mid-off rather than across towards mid-wicket. The front leg now straightens and the body lifts but the head stays down. On some slow turning wickets it can be safer to loft fully than try to drive on the ground, but lofted straight driving can help break up defensive fields.

The most striking example of controlled lofted driving that I can remember was on the initial Cavaliers tour in 1959 at Johannesburg. Hugh Tayfield was bowling tightly for South Africa, when an aging Denis Compton decided to break up his field. A lofted on-drive for six was followed by a straight drive. McGlew pushed out a deep straight hit, whereupon Compton lofted over mid-off. When a deep mid-off was dispatched to the boundary, Compton hit an incredible lofted cover-drive into the crowd. It was impossible to bowl against this or set a field.

Of course Compton was an extraordinarily gifted player, but the lofted drive is available to us all within our own limitations and is used not widely enough.

A final interesting point. How many batsmen, when really going for the bowling, have set themselves to loft the ball only to produce their most scorching carpet-skimming drives? I know many, including myself.

The reason is that on good hard batting wickets, we can afford to drive further away from ourselves, even safely hitting the ball 'on

*All great players are powerful off their legs. Here Doug Walters on-drives.*

the up'. The technique used for imperfect wickets requires the bat to be angled well down when making contact with a drive. This gives you a margin of error, to keep the ball on the ground, and usually means the ball is hit next to your front foot beneath your eyes. On very good wickets, this method can lead to squeezing or killing the drive, which can now be safely and more powerfully hit off deliveries pitching shorter. I would encourage all young batsmen to practise driving 'on the up' on good hard wickets.

## FORWARD DEFENCE

Quite intentionally, I have avoided the discussion of defensive positions until after the outline of attacking methods. Sound defence is essential in batting, but it must be kept in perspective. The aim of batting is to attack, to hit the ball and to score rather than to survive. So the forward defence is introduced only when we find we cannot attack a particular ball.

The aim of the defensive shot is therefore simple. We want a shot that gives least chance of getting out to that particular ball, so that we are still going to be there to attack the next one. Thus the front foot is well forward and towards the ball, the front knee is bent to keep shoulder and head down, the bat and pad are close together, the eye watches the ball right onto the bat, and there is no follow through.

The front shoulder points towards the ball, weight is transferred onto the well-bent front leg, and the full face of the vertical bat is presented to the ball. To do this the top hand must take the bat into the shot ahead of the bottom hand, which grips lightly with thumb and first finger only. To keep the blade vertical, the front elbow must stay well up (for as it drops the bat moves towards the horizontal), and the bottom hand must not grip hard or try to take over.

If you push straight forward, instead of forward and towards the ball, the same problems discussed in driving will occur. You will be too far from off-side deliveries; and for

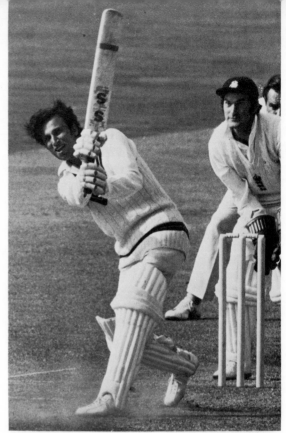

**Top left**   *Barry Richards of South Africa lofts off his toes.*

**Bottom left**   *Another devastating front-foot shot on the on-side—the sweep, performed by Ian Chappell at the Adelaide Oval.*

**Top right**   *Asif Iqbal of Pakistan slams away off his legs.*

**Bottom right**   *Wendy Hills of Western Australia gets in good position and sweeps powerfully.*

*Neil Harvey lofts during an innings in Hong Kong in 1975. Although he had not touched a bat for several years, he stroked the ball perfectly.*

**Top** *Geoff Boycott, leg before wicket to Gleeson, pays the penalty for sweeping off the line of the stumps.*

**Bottom** *The lofted drive is a destructive shot once a batsman has played himself in. Here Keith Stackpole lofts a boundary in an innings of 200 against England.*

on-side deliveries, you will be forced to play around your leg. So once again, don't 'itch' forward in anticipation but wait, make your decision and then move towards the ball.

It is all too easy to become over-dependent on tight front-foot defence. It is difficult for a bowler to penetrate, and therefore very safe for a batsman. But you can become psychologically bogged down by itching forward and so be committed to defence, losing your attacking back-foot shots. *Be careful when you first experiment with 'bat and pad' play; you can overdo it and begin to think of pads before bat as your batting instrument. This is purely negative and there is no future in it.*

Perhaps there are very difficult turning wickets upon which this technique is essential for survival. But on most occasions, what is survival without runs? To adopt the method on hard batting wickets is asking for negative bowling. *Cricket is at its best on the very best batting wickets, when a batsman is trying to score runs, and a bowler is trying to get him out.* A negative approach from either side does the game no good. On a good wicket, when things are in your favour as a batsman, respond by trying to *play shots off both front and back foot.* I wish someone had explained this to me earlier in my own career.

35

# 6  Back-foot Shots

For convenience, I shall discuss the back-foot shots under two sections:

1 Those played with a straight (vertical) bat.

2 Those played with a cross (horizontal) bat.

### STRAIGHT BAT

I have already outlined the fundamentals of these shots in Chapter 4, 'Batting Footwork'. Nevertheless I want to emphasise once more that any player who squares-up chest-on to the bowler when he gets onto the back foot makes it impossible to flow the bat through full-faced and straight onto the ball. To force the ball, he must hit across it, because his body is in the way of a straight bat swing.

If he only used this 'French cricket' position for a defence that had no introductory backlift, he could get away with it. Unfortunately most youngsters who move into that position for any back-foot shot do so for all shots, and it becomes physically impossible to hit with power on the off-side with a vertical bat.

*Back defence* is played to a ball short of a length which you cannot attack. Your back foot moves as far back as possible to give you maximum time to see what the ball has to offer. Although most weight now goes onto the back foot, it is essential to bring back the front foot also to assist balance, for the batsman must not lean back away from the ball. His head should be well forward over the point of contact.

Now because the eye stays above the back foot, its movement is not only back but also towards the ball, so that ball, eye and bat are in one straight line. Thus for a ball outside off-stump, the back foot moves outside off-stump; for a ball in line with middle-stump,

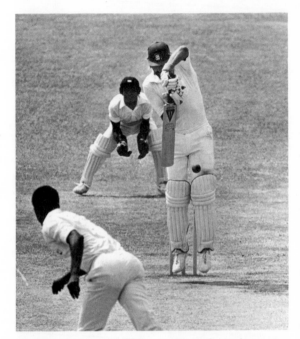

*Graham Gooch defends on the back foot—but not technically correct. Why?*

the foot moves towards middle-stump. Outside leg-stump, however, this principle is not applied as the movement of legs and body in that direction would leave the stumps exposed. Thus for backward defence around leg-stump, the body squares-up to the ball a little more; whilst outside leg-stump, defence is not considered.

But the body only opens up on the leg-side. To keep yourself side-on for all off-side deliveries, the back foot should be placed almost parallel to the crease. The determining factor at all times is that your front shoulder *must* lead towards the ball when you play a vertical bat shot. Where your feet point is only important in that context—you must have your body in such a position that front shoulder leads at the ball. If the ball is well

*Garfield Sobers moves into a back defence position, then hits through the ball to turn defence into attack.*

*Eddie Barlow attacks off the back foot. After hitting the ball, his left leg has come back to retain balance.*

wide of off-stump and your only intention is defence, leave it alone altogether and get your bat well clear, making sure your pads cover the stumps.

Bat and body should remain close together at all times as the blade comes through from a restricted back swing. The top hand stays well ahead of the bottom hand, which grips with thumb and first finger only. There is no follow through and to keep the bat well angled down and vertical requires keeping the front elbow well up.

If the ball kicks unexpectedly, drop the bat below contact if possible, or release your grip. When the rearing ball strikes a bat held firmly, it flies. It is more likely to drop dead from a loosely held bat. It is also worthwhile remembering that a glove is only considered

part of the bat when it is in contact with the bat.

To convert this shot into attack requires an increased backlift, additional power from the bottom hand as the top hand leads the flow of the bat, and a complete follow through. Otherwise the attacking shot is performed similarly to the defensive.

Taller men, such as Miller, O'Neill, Dexter and Greg Chappell, have the advantage here in that they can more easily get over the ball with vertical bat. Smaller men often have to resort to cutting or pulling—shots usually played to shorter deliveries—or they turn their wrists as they make contact with vertical bat, making use of deflection plus the bowler's own pace to compensate for a lack of leverage. In this regard the taller men appear

37

to have a back-foot advantage. Clearly Don Bradman, Lindsay Hassett, Rohan Kanhai, Neil Harvey and other diminutive but great batsmen found an equally successful back-foot method. If you are an ambitious batsman, you must find a method too, for the difference between success and failure in the better grades of cricket can be the ability to score consistently off the back foot. You will find a higher grip will aid your vertical bat shots, since with cocked wrists it will add to your leverage. Those who grip low, or choke the splice, are helping pulls and cuts, but obviate the straight bat variety of back-foot attack.

## CROSS BAT SHOTS

On the off-side of the stumps, these shots are normally the cuts, although shortish off-spinners and medium-pacers can be safely hit through the on-side from anywhere with quick enough eyes and feet. It is pedantic to discourage the pull shot for all but leg-side deliveries.

In perfection the cuttable ball needs to be very short and very wide. The batsman moves his back foot back and across towards the ball with his weight going onto the back foot. Thus he is leaning towards and over the point of contact. He remains side-on.

He must hit at the ball hard—a snick will still take some catching—but roll the wrists over the ball to hit it down, before following through. If the bat comes from a higher position down onto the ball, your chances of keeping it down are better. Thus a high backlift aids the shot.

In modern cricket, the combination of brilliant close to the wicket fieldsmen and 'umbrella' fields can make cutting hazardous—so many 'good shots' have been

**Top** *Ian Redpath moves all weight onto the back foot as he cuts.*

*Doug Walters cuts during a century against the West Indies. When set, he cut attacks to ribbons.*

*Ian Chappell demonstrates the hook shot. As the right foot goes back and across he squares-up, 'chest-on'. The backlift is high. Square-on and inside the ball he hits through firmly, wrists rolling the bat over the ball to keep it down. He follows through, still perfectly balanced.*

39

caught. Jimmy Burke has assured me that were he commencing his career now, he would reverse his approach to cutting pace bowlers and *cut up*. An up-angled bat to pace finds those gaps behind slips, and although such 'upper-cuts' may cause shudders amongst purists, they are destructive and perhaps safer than normal down cutting. Eddie Barlow certainly utilised the shot most effectively.

On slower wickets many players become perpetual cutters, dispatching anything even slightly short of a length. Many of these players also back-pedal outside leg-stump to 'give themselves room' and cut closer to off-stump. Colin McDonald, for instance, must have scored half his runs cutting, many of those off his stumps; whilst Neil Dansie on the Adelaide Oval, where square boundaries are very short and wickets very slow, seemed to cut or pull even half volleys. But from a youngster's point of view, it is preferable to cut at the wider, shorter ball and try to develop back-foot attack with a straight bat for balls lined closer to the stumps.

Towards the on-side, your cross bat back-foot shots are the *pull and the hook. The pull shot I define as that hit off the line of your body* forward of square-leg from slow bowling, medium-pace bowling or an apology for pace bowling. The ball is short-pitched anywhere from outside off-stump to leg-stump.

The back foot moves back and across towards off-stump and the other foot follows back but outside the line of leg-stump. You have now turned chest-on to the bowler, feet separated across your stumps, and with body weight forward. A full cross bat swing with extended arms comes down from a high backlift to *pick up* the ball in front of the eyes.

Normally wrists roll over the ball to keep it down, but frequently you may wish to loft it. I must stress that you are really hitting into the pull shot hard, intercepting the flight of the ball to crash it through mid-wicket. The bottom hand is clubbing hard, as you play a true baseball drive.

*Mike Denness pulls Bishen Bedi off the line of the stumps. He has chosen to loft the ball to clear the in-field.*

When wickets are a little damp, bowlers frequently set close fields hoping for chances from the popping ball. Too many bowlers in these conditions drop short, however. They should be well up, forcing you to play forward or even to drive. But they enjoy seeing their deliveries jump and/or turn, and so drop a fraction short. The forward playing batsman is in real trouble, but because conditions are unsuited to driving, you should be itching to get on the back foot now. Anything that drops the slightest bit short—particularly from the medium-pacer or off-spinner—can be murdered through mid-wicket no matter what line it is bowled along.

The *hook shot* is an entirely different proposition, and in fact few players are even in the position where they need to execute a true hook shot. For the hook is played to a pacey delivery rising chest or head height, and seldom are wickets firm enough or bowlers fast enough to bowl such deliveries anywhere outside of first-class cricket. In club and grade cricket, the majority of so-called bumpers are long hops and can be safely dispatched with the pull shot.

No player can consistently pull real pace, however. If he leaves his body in line with the ball depending on his cross bat pull for continued physical safety, he must be 'cleaned up' eventually. Real pace covers the 20 metres in less than a second—in which time the batsman must see the ball, judge the length and bounce, position himself and then hit it. Even if the player is setting himself for the shot in advance, this is simply asking too much of human reaction time. Therefore, for the hook shot, *he must get his body inside the line of the ball* as a safety precaution. This does not mean scurrying a metre inside the line, but instead of being hit in front of the eyes, the ball is contacted just wide of the eyes.

Against normal pace bowling, the in-form batsman can get inside the line of the ball quickly and play his hook shot—almost certainly backward of square. Some batsmen, in swaying back on the back foot, lean away from the ball and consistently hook up.

*Geoff Boycott has tried to keep the ball down by rolling his wrists, but eye positions seem to indicate that the ball is in the air. This can happen when the ball gets onto you a little quicker than expected.*

41

Others position both feet, keep the shoulders level and, by rolling the wrists over the ball, keep it down. But either way, footwork is much the same as the pull.

Those players who have encountered real pace or have struck normal pace on very fast wickets realise that consistent and safe hooking is then impossible. The player who has got away with pull technique under easier conditions is in real physical danger; the correct hooker—who is often a compulsive reflex hooker—can score runs but with every chance of dismissal; whilst the majority of players are forced to resort to evasive tactics.

In first-class cricket, such evasive techniques are very important. Particularly in the countries that produce hard wickets, the bumper becomes an integral part of any attack, whilst countering the bumper is a major part of batsmanship. An inability to cope with bumpers gives a specialist batsman little chance of success in first-class cricket. News of his problem travels fast and he seldom faces anything else but pace, whilst his discomfort continues to show.

The evasive footwork is different to that of the hook shot. The batsman still moves the back foot back and across towards off-stump, but does not square-up so completely, tending to stay more side-on and swaying inside or outside the ball from *the pivot of a bent back leg.*

Whatever happens, your eye should not be taken from the ball. If you do make an initial error of judgement, only quick reflexes and eyesight can get you out of trouble. *Any form of ducking that leads to losing sight of the ball is poor technique and dangerous.* Tom Graveny insists that never taking your eyes off the ball is the number one rule for playing bouncers. 'If you keep on watching it,' he said, recalling a duel with Charlie Griffiths, 'something can save you, no matter how late!.'

More and more players move into a hook shot position with no intention of hooking, and then try to get out of the way. Now they are chest-on, where sideways swaying is

limited and evasion is restricted to a head forward duck—very dangerous!

Fortunately, because the true bumper is usually limited to first-class cricket, only talented players of some experience are asked to combat it. Yet, although skill avoids accidents, most first-class batsmen in Australia eventually reach a stage where bumpers find flaws in an otherwise sound technique. Whether their eyes or movements become slower, or whether they become more aware of the dangers involved, the fact remains that their confidence and enthusiasm against the quicks declines. This is one of the reasons for the early departure of many top-class Australian batsmen from the first-class scene. A pity!

Even though they are unlikely to need it, is still valuable for youngsters to practise the technique for countering the bumper, as well as hooking and pulling. If at an early stage they can learn the simple footwork and the immense importance of the bent back leg pivot that controls a side-on sway, they have priceless experience to call upon if necessary.

The cuts, the pull and hook shots can be well taught using a tennis ball because you can obtain adequate bounce without great pace. Throwing a ball at an appropriate spot to obtain the lift desired allows all the shots to be practised either indoors or outdoors.

I remember opening the batting for New South Wales and spending half an hour or so against a bowling machine on several occasions. It was set for bumpers at full pace—which, I am told, is well over 160 km/h—and although most of the time I faced it without a bat to test my evasive footwork, never did it present the problems of a Frank Tyson, Wes Hall or Charlie Griffiths.

Finally, for the coach! Encourage all batsmen to try and develop power in their back-foot shots. Try to get them to flow the bat through, trying to hit the ball through the field towards cover and mid-wicket or even straight.

The shots have been discussed, their requirements analysed. Most coaches will try to iron out errors as youngsters perform the shots at practice or after matches. Another thoroughly worthwhile exercise, which captures youthful imagination, is to equip the entire team with a bat, or a bat substitute such as a stump. Go through all the back-foot shots one day; another time the front foot. Then separate the young players well apart and persuade them to play an imaginary knock. Nominate the innings shot by shot at first, then leave it to them. With younger boys in particular, it will do your heart good to see them absorbed in carving up that opposition attack, which upon investigation is usually comprised of Lillee, Thomson, Underwood and the like.

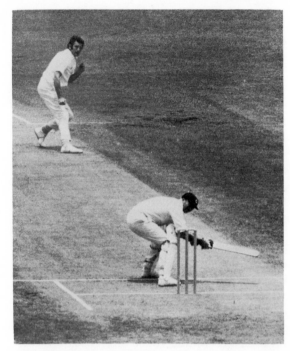

*Sam Trimble ducks under a Snow bouncer. He is balanced and controlled, but it is doubtful if he saw the ball before it reached him.*

*Tony Steele of New South Wales has his feet in good position, but the forward 'blind' ducking is potentially dangerous.*

# SECTION II   BOWLING
# 7   Fundamentals of Bowling

Generally speaking, the basis of bowling is accuracy.

## 1  Accuracy

This will be achieved if:

(a) Your *approach, delivery* and *follow through* are not so incorrect that they handicap you. The orthodox methods are discussed in the following pages, but it is certainly not necessary to meet all of these requirements exactly to be a successful bowler.

(b) You *concentrate* hard and stare at your target.

(c) You *practise* sensibly, hard, often and correctly. Practice does not make perfect unless (a) + (b) + (c) apply.

(d) You obtain and take advantage of opportunities to *bowl in match conditions*.

(e) You have adequate *natural ability, temperament* and *determination*.

When you have achieved accuracy, or as you are achieving it, you are able to utilise the other two skills of bowling.

## 2  Variation

Accuracy without any variation is not enough; your bowling becomes too mechanical and predictable. On the other hand, variation without accuracy is completely useless.

The variations, large and small, available to all types of bowlers are discussed in the following pages. Keep on talking amongst fellow players, however, and keep on experimenting for yourself.

## 3  Bowling to Different Batsmen in Different Conditions

Once you have accuracy and variation, you are able to bowl the required delivery to the particular batsman.

This entails the recognition of batting strengths and weaknesses and how to use these; the summing up of wicket, weather and match conditions. This is the real 'art' of bowling, and although much of it will probably only come with personal experience, you will learn more quickly if you watch, talk and read about the game as widely as possible.

This chapter sets out to give you some ideas on these fundamentals of bowling.

## FUNDAMENTALS

Bowlers and fieldsmen win matches. Any team that consistently dismisses the opposition cheaply is a winner. The skills of bowling cannot be discussed briefly. Each type requires its own qualities, techniques and attitudes, and I discuss these in the three following chapters.

Several factors, however, are essential for all bowlers. First, a bowler *must love bowling and thrive on lots of it*—the more the better. All bowlers develop greatly when given responsibility, mainly because acceptance as a front-rank bowler ensures consistent use. If you don't enjoy bowling for hours, you'll probably never be an outstanding bowler. I remember Richie Benaud and Alec Bedser as

44

*Garfield Sobers in a classical side-on delivery position. Note the back foot parallel to crease; the front arm high reaching and the position of head and eyes.*

Graham Mackenzie in the 'cradle' position. Weight is transferring from right foot to left, but the bowler remains side-on to the batsman.

**Left** Greg Chappell in a classical side-on position.

**Below** Eddie Barlow follows through. Compare the other photographs of follow throughs in this chapter.

Dayle Hadlee of New Zealand illustrates the moment just before delivery. All the weight is now on the front foot, the left side is braced and the left arm has dropped down.

the hardest workers at practice I have ever seen; for them a bowling work-out often meant three or four hours straight. The section in this chapter on spin bowling discusses ways in which you can vary long bowling practices in order to retain concentration.

The second is also an important factor—*concentration*. Concentration is always stressed as an essential in batting, but is too often overlooked in bowling. Yet concentration is at least half of the bowling game.

Another essential is the *temperament to develop a philosophical approach to bowling*. A bowler must learn to enjoy bowling well as much as taking wickets. Often he will bowl well without wickets, but if he continues to bowl well, the wickets must come. Sometimes he will bowl badly and take wickets, but this cannot last. It is a matter of accepting reality. Of course the happiest alternative is to bowl well and take wickets, but this will not always happen. The bowler must accept the disappointments and occasional 'thrashings' as an integral part of his game—but not too often!

A bowler also needs to *think about his art*. He must talk with others, listen, read, watch and experiment. He must remember that he can always continue to learn.

Finally, there are some *basic mechanical requirements* such as approach, delivery and follow through which require consideration and practice. These are dealt with in the following chapters, but from a beginner's point of view they are dealt with exceptionally well by Martin Horton in his *New Zealand Coaching Manual*. With his permission I set out these ideas:

*Position one:* Just before his delivery stride the bowler should land so that his right foot is parallel to the bowling crease; his bowling arm should be starting its swing from as high as possible, usually from near his mouth, and the left arm will be pointing and stretching out towards the target he is aiming for. At this stage the body will be leaning back, especially in the case of the quicker bowlers. It is important that the bowler is looking at the target over the back of his left arm, as this will enable him to get much more body action.

*Position two:* By now the bowler will have turned completely sideways to the batsman, and will be arching back and away from the target. The left foot will have come through and landed so that it is pointing approximately in the direction of the batsman, although this will vary slightly according to what sort of ball is to be delivered. The bowling arm has started to drop in its final swing. This position is the finish of the winding-up process and it is most important that the bowler doesn't let himself get too square-on at this moment.

*Position three:* This is sometimes called the cradle position and is the halfway stage in the delivery. The body weight is in the process of transferring from the right foot to the left, but the bowler is still turned sideways to the batsman as much as possible. Whatever happens, the right shoulder must not start to come through too soon, otherwise the bowler will lose both pace and accuracy.

*Position four:* The moment of delivery. All the weight is now on the left or front foot with the bowling arm as high as possible, especially in the case of the in-swinger. The left side is braced so that the bowler has something to bowl against. The front or left arm has dropped right down, but care should be taken to make sure that it comes down straight and therefore doesn't pull the front shoulder off-line.

*Position five:* This is the follow through. The young bowler may ask himself why this is so important as he has already let the ball go, but unless he has a proper finish to his action it is obvious that he hasn't used his body efficiently, and hasn't put all he's got into the delivery. The bowler should follow through as far as is necessary for him to complete his delivery smoothly. The bowling arm will have swung right down somewhere near the left knee, although this will vary according to the pace and the type of bowler. To assist this the

left arm swings back and up so that it is pointing directly behind the bowler.

Occasionally the coach will find a bowler who cannot bowl at all but would like to. It is usually best to start him in the third position of the basic bowling action and let him stand at the crease and rock or lob the ball down the wickets to a partner. This can be done indoors in the gym.

But now let me go on to the specialised fields within the bowling arts.

## SPIN BOWLING

The concept behind spin bowling is a simple one. If you spin the ball with fingers and wrist in a clockwise direction (or left to right), the ball spins through the air in that direction, and turns off the pitch in that direction. You have created off-spin. On the other hand, anti-clockwise (or right to left) spin by fingers and wrist creates that direction of spin through the air, and the ball turns from the left. This is leg-spin.

Bowlers can make spins more difficult to detect by practice but the basics remain. The clockwise spin through the air must be off-spin and vice versa. Therefore no cricketer should be hopelessly confused by any spinner. If he understands the mechanics of bowling, then watches carefully the bowler's hand and the spin through the air, nothing is mysterious. If he applies his mind to the problem everything is logical.

The wrong'un is a perfectly logical delivery for example. If you investigate how it is bowled and spend a little time bowling it yourself, you should seldom be deceived by this delivery, and certainly not be tricked twice by the same bowler. If a bowler does deceive you, work out what he must have done and carefully watch him bowl. Don't

*This series of photographs shows the approach, delivery and follow through of Bob Massie.*

allow yourself to shrug off the deception, for that way you are failing to build your experience. John Gleeson is a bowler whose mechanics must be understood in order to read him. Both the wrong'un and the Gleeson method are discussed in Chapters 9 and 10.

Many batsmen debate the virtues of 'picking a bowler' from the hand, in the air, or off the pitch. This is not the place to enter such an argument, but it seems a clear advantage for the batsman to see something from the hand as this gives more time, although I realise that 'reading a bowler' does not necessarily stop you getting out. More importantly, for the 'real' cricketer understanding, performing and recognising any delivery is simply part of his education. He is restless until he can read each bowler. For this reason my advice on spin bowling is aimed not only at bowlers, but to all those who want to 'learn cricket'.

*Wrist-spinning* refers to right hand leg-break and left arm off-break bowlers who use the leverage of fingers and wrist to create their spin. For convenience most of the discussion applies to right arm leg-spinners but the left armer can logically adapt these comments for his own use.

*Finger-spinning* refers to right arm off-spinners and left arm leg-spinners with the majority of comments mentioning the former.

(In fact wrist-spinners should also use their fingers, whilst finger-spinners must use the wrist, but let's not get bogged down in the common sense of cricketing terminology.) Certainly both types of bowlers have different skills, different attributes, advantages, disadvantages and, particularly, different mental approaches. Wrist-spin is dealt with in Chapter 9, finger-spin in Chapter 10.

# 8    Seam and Pace

In discussing swing we must clarify our terms of reference. An out-swinger is always the ball that moves from a right hand batsman's leg-side towards off, whether it pitches outside leg-stump or off-stump. On the other hand, the in-swinger moves from a right hand batsman's off to leg.

So you want to be a pace bowler? Which young cricketer at some time has not felt the urge to hurl them down with fire and pace and bounce? Probably though, unless you have the physical attributes necessary for such onerous work, your potential in speed is limited. You may end up as the medium-pacer who needs the subtleties of swing and cut to make up for that lack of blistering pace.

## THE SEAM EFFECT AND SWING

But whether fast, fast-medium, or gentle medium-pace, you must come to understand the significance of those stitches on the leather ball—the *seam*. To begin with, you must have the *three-finger grip* with index and middle fingers atop the seam and thumb beneath, whilst fingers four and five relax folded as balancers.

You can experiment with grips for different deliveries, but the three-finger grip is basic. Why? Because your aim must be to propel the ball through the air with a vertical seam rotating as evenly as possible. You must try to eliminate a wobbling seam, or one that lies over either way—it should be *even and upright*. Your best method of perfecting this is by delivering the ball over 5 to 8 metres to a friend. Over such a short distance you can clearly see the seam's rotation yourself. But make sure that even a delivery over 5 to 8 metres is done with a full action—one pace to delivery position, use of both arms and follow

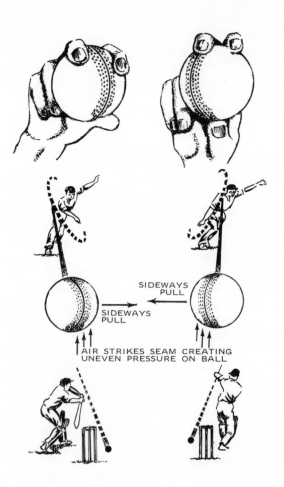

*This diagram illustrates the grip, action and seam effect that create out-swing (on the left) and in-swing (on the right).*

through. Don't simply stand chest-on and roll your arm over.

And why the emphasis on upright and even rotation? Let me explain this way. Imagine a twenty cent piece as the seam of a mini-cricket ball with both rounded sides removed. If you hold the coin with the three-finger grip and deliver it to achieve upright and even rotation, nine times out of ten it will deviate from its course in the air—that is, it will 'swing'. Which way it will swing is dependent upon your method of delivery. Every individual has a natural swing one way or the other. (It is a simple matter to recognise the natural swing by watching a few deliveries from each bowler—but more of that later.)

The coin will 'swing' because nine times out of ten it will not be propelled straight ahead. If it points slightly towards the off-side of the wicket, wind pressure on the face of the coin forces it towards the off—it swings 'out'. If the coin is delivered slightly towards the on-side 'in' swing is created in the same way.

If the coin wobbles or lies down, the seam effect is lost and no swing results. On a windless day the coin will still swing when even and upright, as it creates its own breeze moving through the air. Even the slowest of bowlers bowls at over fifty kilometres per hour. Clearly however, breeze from the on will aid 'out-swing' and vice versa.

The cricket ball experiences this same 'twenty cent' effect despite its rounded sides. When the ball is new the seam is more pronounced and with 'even upright seam' any youngster will swing it naturally one way or the other dependent on his action. As the ball becomes older the seam is flattened a little, but shine on one side of the ball partly compensates for this. A simple unscientific explanation is that we place the shinier side on the leg-side (that is, on-side of course), wind resistance slips off it, but grips on the rougher side, thus aiding the seam effect to create out-swing. Remember, the shine won't help without seam effect, and the shine should be placed on the opposite side to the way you want the ball to go. Those bowlers polishing

*Mike Procter of South Africa illustrates the most important factor in seam bowling. The seam must be released rotating evenly and upright.*

away on their creams are only working on one side repairing any small cuts or 'bruises' with 'spit and polish' to retain a completely smooth and relatively friction-free surface. When both shine and seam have gone, then, under normal circumstances, the ball's swing days are over.

**Above** *Dennis Lillee, in the early days of his career, illustrates approach, delivery and follow through.*

**Left** *Clearly Max Walker has bowled an inswinger. Look at the angle of the seam leaving his hand.*

It is the duty of the pace bowler to shine the ball. A little spit and polish will repair bruises and the bowler must work on the ball to retain shine, particularly nowadays since legislation denies other fieldsmen the polishing role. The fieldsmen who needlessly allow the new ball to go to ground and throw returns to the keeper into the dirt are ignoring their team's interests. The ball must be returned to keeper or bowler with due consideration of many factors that are discussed later, but an important factor is conserving shine on the ball. A well-drilled and knowledgeable team is apparent when it is fielding and bowling in wet conditions. Then each player must do all he can to stop water entering the seam, for

once this happens the ball swells, loses shape and is as easy to bowl as a piece of soap. The ball is carefully dried by everyone, particularly around the seam, and never touches the ground except when it must.

The South Africans are the players most concerned with ball conservation. It always astonished me over there to find a better-than-new ball with the score over 200. But patch and polish, polish, polish by all the players held the shine—no wonder pace and seam has become the basis of their attack. They are not looking for spin, when swing and cut are always there.

But even if a ball has mirror-like shine, or a seam like a discus, it will not swing without the even upright rotation mentioned before. Watching Keith Miller in action always emphasised this. I remember Keith bowling on a Sydney Cricket Ground greentop in the mid-1950s against South Australia. From slip, the whole strip of the vertical seam was more apparent than I can ever recall. His

beautifully high delivery and strong wrist flick ensured even upright rotation.

That day the ball 'did everything'. South Australia were dismissed for less than thirty, Gil Langley top scoring with twelve. Miller took seven for twelve and, if I remember rightly, South Australian opener, Dave Harris, had the dubious fame of making a pair before lunch on Saturday.

## IN-SWING OR OUT-SWING

So you have practised the three-finger grip; you are delivering the ball consistently with an even and upright seam rotation; you are polishing away on one side of the ball. Why do some swing naturally 'out', others 'in'?

An out-swing bowler delivers the ball with first and second fingers pushing straight behind the seam in the direction it is pointing. The seam should point 'just-off' straight ahead, that is, for the out-swinger, towards first slip. Turning the seam around further—

53

say, towards gully slip—does not increase swing; on the contrary this counteracts upright rotation, and swing is gone.

The fingers should not cut either inside or outside the ball for swing, as this too will upset even and upright rotation. The palm of your hand within the three-finger grip will face towards the direction of swing. For the out-swinger, the bowler requires a pro-nounced *side-on* position. To achieve such a position, the bowler's back foot is, in perfection, almost parallel to the bowling crease, whilst the front foot is closer to the line of the stumps than the back foot. The left arm is extended, reaching high, with the bowler eyeing his target 'outside' the arm. Such a position is far more difficult to achieve than 'chest-on' to the batsman, and demands suppleness and litheness in the fast bowlers. But for late out-swing and for full body action as a whole, it is a very great advantage.

Indeed it cannot be over-emphasised that cricket is a side-on game. Whether batting, returning the ball to the keeper, or bowling— a cricketer has an advantage if his shoulder (and from a right hander's point of view, this is his left shoulder of course), rather than his chest, points towards his objective.

In a side-on delivery position the natural arc of the bowling arm can be thought of as a portion of the rotation of a wheel revolving from the direction of the umpire towards first slip. The higher your arm, the greater the bounce and the later swing is likely to be. This arc, coupled with the cutting away of the left arm and a full body swing and wrist flick at delivery, will work with correct seam, finger and palm position to create out-swing. The arm continues naturally so that the right hand follows through around the vicinity of the left hip pocket.

On the other hand, the natural in-swing bowler is usually more chest-on to the batsman, with his feet pointing more towards the batsman. His arm comes over closer to the head, the first and second fingers and the palm of the hand push straight behind a seam facing leg-slip—they cut neither inside nor

outside the ball but push straight. The follow through of the hand comes closer to the left knee—but certainly does not go to the right of the right knee as theory once had it. Once again the seam needs only to be 'just off' straight ahead; the three-finger grip is basic; and the shinier side is on the opposite side to the way you want it to go.

All bowlers are by nature closer to one of these actions than the other. Watch a youngster bowl an over with the three-finger grip, and you will clearly see which is his natural swing. Consistent rotation of the seam in the direction of slips reveals a natural in-swing. With knowledge of why a ball swings, and how he can go about it, the rest is up to him. Most young players will be moving the ball one way or the other within ten minutes' work.

The question then arises—how to go about bowling 'the other one', the swinger that is not natural? The bowler simply copies the features of the opposite delivery. As a natural out-swinger, in order to bowl the in-swing, he must square-up his delivery position a little through changing the position of feet, chest and left arm; adapt the grip and shiny side; and note the changed follow through. With practice, the change necessary lessens. But still the basic essentials remain—the three-finger grip plus even upright seam rotation.

Some bowlers need to turn their action around more than others to achieve the opposite swing. I remember vividly, whilst coaching in the Transvaal in 1962, watching Eddie Barlow bowling in-swingers with an exaggerated wrist turn which to me indicated he was a natural out-swing bowler. Let me explain! If you need to turn your wrist right around inside the ball with an obviously exaggerated movement in order to push the seam towards fine leg, you have come from a natural out-swing position. We chatted together, and he began to experiment with his more natural ball, the out-swinger. It added greatly to his pace and 'devil', and as far as I know he has continued to bowl them since.

*I seriously question the wisdom of a*

*Graham Mackenzie was a classically side-on bowler.*

*Len Pascoe quickly established himself in first-class cricket. Check his technique in these four shots.*

*youngster with a promising out-swinger being encouraged to bowl the in-swinger—or vice versa. Certainly he should know how it works and how he can do it—and at times he can play around with it—but I feel he is better off perfecting his natural ball. Variation can be obtained with the off-cutter which is so much closer to his out-swing action, and he can leave the in-swing until later in his career when his action is consolidated beyond fear of upset.* After all, I suppose the majority of pace bowlers have only swung the ball one way.

Let's recheck. Three-finger grip, even upright seam, no wobbling, shine on the opposite side to the intended direction of swing. Practise over 5 to 8 metres, carefully checking the seam's rotation, using a cricket ball with a well-defined seam, a twenty cent piece, the lid of some tin, or preferably a piece of 2-centimetre timber cut to the same

diameter as a cricket ball. When you are delivering nine out of ten with perfect even rotation, we shall go on!

## YOUR APPROACH AND DELIVERY

We shall assume that you have tried to achieve the side-on delivery position with the footwork mentioned. Your left arm is reaching high to lift your body to full stretch and you are eyeing your target from the off-side of your arm (assuming right hand bowlers to right hand batsmen).

To achieve such a classical delivery will need work, and fitting this delivery smoothly onto your approach will need more work still. How far you run is really up to you alone. You must judge from your length of stride and your requirements in reaching top speed. But generally most young players run too far.

Frequently with very long approaches, the stride is lost and the entire run-up wasted. Skipping and hopping, shortening and

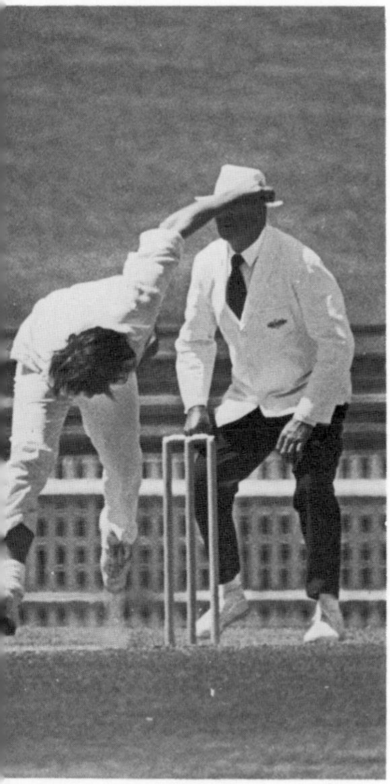

*Fred Trueman was one of England's greatest fast bowlers. A classical action, real pace, great accuracy and control of swing—he had them all.*

lengthening of stride, are all indications of misjudged run-up—and the longer the approach, the greater the margin for error. Too many young players are running for the sake of running, perhaps hoping to demoralise the batsman, but usually only tiring themselves and decreasing their effectiveness.

I don't mean that all youngsters should attempt to bowl fast from a ten-pace run. Not at all, it is an individual matter. But thirty paces is ridiculous from every point of view—and particularly from that of time wastage. Indeed time limits on overs may not be far away if fast bowlers continue to take advantage of long runs to slow the game down.

You need an approach in which you can build up from a comfortable jog to a moment of maximum momentum at delivery. Watching film of Lillee or Thomson can teach you more about this aspect than any written words. Practise by pacing out a run-up with an observer helping you. Start your approach, building up speed into delivery without watching the bowling crease, or footmarks at any stage. Your eyes look down to see that your first step begins exactly at the same spot you have marked for every ball bowled. But after this first check, your eyes remain fixed on target. Many youngsters don't really know what they are looking at, and tend to bowl vaguely towards the other end.

Clearly your target is the place you are trying to bowl the ball, so you certainly don't need to watch the batsman. Draw an imaginary line from yourself to the position (or 'line') you wish to attack. Concentrate throughout the run-up to watch this line. To do so your head and eyes should remain perfectly steady throughout the approach,

and it's not a bad idea to keep the shoulders steady too.

Later you may attempt to bowl at a chosen 'spot', but to begin with a 'line' will do. Any bowler who can bowl a good line—even if he can do nothing else—will be a very popular one with his captain and team.

Now back to your approach. You are not worried about no-balling at this stage, as your sole aim is to develop a comfortable stride which can be repeated exactly ball after ball. *It is damaging for a coach to correct each no-ball at this stage as the stride is constantly interfered with.* Frankly I don't concern myself over a youngster bowling no-balls in practice conditions, as long as he can get back

*Dennis Lillee developed into one of the greatest fast bowlers of all time. These photographs help tell the story of fast bowling. They show the balance and co-ordination, the power, the determination, the enthusiasm and the immense physical effort involved.*

when you ask him to concentrate on doing so.

Once the approach has settled after practice, the observer helps. Perhaps the bowler is consistently no-balling or wastes a metre. As long as the bowler has practised to ignore crease and stumps at the bowler's end, the adjustment to length of run-up is a simple matter. He is running a given distance with a given stride, and where he begins and ends is of little consequence. So he simply begins a metre closer or further back.

As your relaxed accelerating approach develops, you are running chest-on towards the batsman with bowling wrist flapping relaxed at your side. Yet at delivery I have stressed the side-on position. Obviously in the final paces before delivery the body is forced around by the positioning of feet. The turn is not made in the final two paces alone, however, as this puts too great a strain on the accelerating body. Of course it is easier to continue your approach straight ahead, chest-on, toes pointing towards the batsman, but in so doing you are losing body action and tending to bowl with your right arm alone.

Many bowlers achieve the side-on delivery position by hard practice, then waste their lead-up work by allowing the left arm to cut away too early. This drags them chest-on once more, throwing the body away from the delivery as it falls away off balance towards cover. That left arm needs to remain tucked into the ribs until the ball is well on its way. Now the body follows through behind the delivery towards slips, and continues to follow through naturally as far as it wants to go. Do not force an exaggerated follow through that could divert your concentration; on the other hand, an abrupt halt after delivery will limit your effectiveness. Once again let me stress that word concentration, for many overlook that it is the basis of bowling just as it is the basis of batting.

Out-swing bowlers attempt to get in close to the stumps at the bowler's end for their delivery. This gives the angle to accentuate out-swing. These bowlers, in attempting to achieve correct technique, are sometimes warned for running down the wicket. This has happened more often over the last few years since the front-foot no-ball rule, and many bowlers have suffered (as they usually do from cricketing legislation). Grahame Corling with his lovely side-on, close to the stumps, out-swing action was upset greatly by this rule, losing confidence and eventually his out-swinger. If you are unfortunate enough to experience this, your answer must not be squaring-up your action and allowing your follow through to fall away off the pitch—it can only be by going wider on the bowling crease, sad as this may be.

## VARIATIONS IN YOUR SEAM ATTACK

Just as the out-swing bowler tries to get in as close to the stumps as possible at delivery, so the in-swing bowler usually comes from wide on the return crease to accentuate his angle. But of course the seamer will not rigidly adhere to these crease positions for in-swing and out-swing, for the variation of delivery position along the bowling crease is a basic bowling strategy. Most top bowlers use only two or three different positions along the crease, however, as constantly varying it could upset your approach, and makes it difficult for you to concentrate on your stock ball. And without a stock ball you have nothing to build variations on. The stock ball is your natural delivery and should be as accurate as possible.

There is no need to bowl everything in order to be a top-class seam bowler. First of all you need to be able to bowl accurately to a field, although for cricket's sake you should avoid bowling short of a length to defensive fields. I hope you will choose to bowl aggressively, to be constantly trying to get the batsman out, rather than bowling to defensive fields in order to 'bore' him out. Later you may bowl at a spot, but early in your career begin by bowling on a line—that is, along the line of the off-stump or whatever line of attack you decide is necessary.

I'll assume by now that you have discovered which is your natural swing. Let's imagine that an out-swinger is your natural ball and that your most comfortable pace is fast-medium. A fine attacking over from you does not require a collection of in-swingers, out-swingers, cutters and slower balls—not at all! Here is a theoretical over.

Ball one—your natural out-swinger from close to the stumps, along the line of the off-stump, at normal pace—your stock ball.

Ball two—the same.

Ball three—out-swinger from wider on the crease, hurled down as fast as possible, well up but wider of the off-stump.

Ball four—out-swinger from close to stumps, well within normal speed, at off-stump.

Ball five—normal pace, close to stumps, off-cutter or straight ball.

Ball six—top pace at off-stump, but dug in to gain lift.

Ball seven—normal pace from wider on return crease, with no swing.

Ball eight—stock ball.

There is a varied over, yet most of it comes from use of crease and slight variations of pace—with emphasis on 'slight', as the best change of pace is barely detectable. Accuracy is assumed, but otherwise only your normal delivery plus a straight ball or off-cutter is required.

Of course you must not imagine that each over is decided in advance mechanically as above. Sometimes you may bowl this way, but usually you have the variations up your sleeve and produce them to attack each batsman as required. You try to sum him up, bowl to his weaknesses, working on him over a period of time. It may be that to some batsman eight out-swingers, well-up, outside off-stump are your best means of attack. What I am trying to get at is simply that you don't need to bowl the whole bag of tricks to be a capable seam bowler.

Of course some players are able to introduce a great deal of variety into a total plan without loss of accuracy. Alan Conolly began his career as an out and out speedster

*Not all successful bowlers are copy-book. These photographs clearly show the unorthodoxy of Max Walker and Bob Willis, two highly successful Test bowlers.*

who relied on pace and vigour to gain his wickets. He was a fine opening bowler who 'got into you', bowling aggressively, retaining his pace and never giving in. But in recent times Alan has shortened his approach, dropped his pace somewhat, and gained subtlety.

He bowls both in-swinger and out-swinger, a good off-cutter and several well-disguised slower balls. He varies his pace cleverly and can still produce a really good bumper out of the blue. In addition, his perfect accuracy, intelligent appraisal of opponents, strength and determination have made him one of the world's finest medium-fast bowlers since World War II. He is of course Victoria's greatest wicket-taker ever in interstate cricket.

Geoff Noblet from South Australia was another seam bowler with a wide variety of deliveries. To variations of swing and pace he added a vicious off-spinner. Delivered like a baseball pitcher's out-curve drop, this delivery bit and reared. I only faced Geoff at the end of his career, but on Lancashire League wickets he was the most devastating medium-fast bowler I have batted against.

But these two are exceptions. The majority of seamers do not have that kind of variety and can do very well without it, as long as they use intelligently what they do have.

## CUTTING THE BALL AND EXPERIMENTATION

The terms 'off-cutter' and 'leg-cutter' have been used frequently without adequate explanation. Whereas the pace bowlers move the ball in the air with seam effect as described, they are also able to make the ball deviate off the pitch by a limited spin movement called 'cut'.

Frequently late swing causes a ball to move off the pitch. Some bowlers, too, try to deliver

*These magnificent shots illustrate the power and strength of Charles Griffiths. There was controversy about his action but none about his pace.*

an even upright seam hoping the ball will deviate from the pitch off the seam. This happens more on the lush greenery of English and New Zealand wickets than on the baked wickets of hotter countries.

But these two types of movement are not 'cutters', for the cutter is not relying on the seam effect at all. The off-cutter is halfway between an out-swinger and an off-break; and a leg-cutter halfway between an in-swinger and a leg-break. Let me explain.

For the out-swinger, fingers continue straight behind the seam pushing it along the line of swing. The fingers must not cut away on either side of the ball, or even upright seam is lost. For the off-break, all fingers (particularly the index finger), thumb and the wrist snap outside the ball to create left to right spin. For the off-cutter the two top fingers of the three-finger grip cut across the ball from left to right but the thumb beneath moves very little, whilst wrist-spin motion is negligible.

One way to bowl the off-cutter is to hold it the same as the out-swinger, but deliver it with the two top fingers on the outside of the ball instead of on top. Some adjust the three-finger grip. The thumb is taken off the seam and brought halfway up the closer half of the ball. The index finger stays atop the seam, whilst the second finger drops down the outer half of the ball. Whatever grip, the bowler must practise to cut those two, top fingers sharply outside the ball.

Clearly the off-cutter is closer to the out-swing action and is perfect variation for this bowler. The out-swing goes away in the air; the off-cutter comes back in off the pitch. The leg-cutter is the more natural and sensible variation for a natural in-swinger.

By all means, then, practise cutting just as you practise to perfect your seam work. As well, look for something new, experimenting with grips and ideas. There are still secrets of bowling to be discovered, and if you are the first to discover one, you could follow in the footsteps of such innovators as Bosanquet or Iverson.

The different methods used to bowl a slower ball without changing the pace of the arm are interesting examples to experiment with. For instance, Alan Conolly bowled two slower balls:

1 His own special, the 'knuckle ball'. A baseball pitcher's variation, Alan introduced it into his bowling. His huge fingers bent up behind the ball, and at delivery he straightened and flicked these fingers. This created over-spin on the ball and caused it to loop and bounce.

2 The half-ball grip—a more orthodox delivery. Instead of the normal out-swing grip with a finger on either side of the seam and thumb beneath on the seam, the grip is transferred to be on the outer half of the ball only. Thus with a normal delivery, the ball slips out between thumb and index finger as an off-spinning slower ball.

Ray Lindwall did much the same, but retained the exact out-swing grip with index finger lifted off the ball. The result is similar to the half-ball grip. Neil Hawke used the lifted finger also to obtain a half-ball effect. But because he was a natural in-swinger, it was his second finger lifted from the seam, and the ball slipped out on the other side of the index finger. This is very difficult to achieve if you are a natural out-swing bowler.

Finally, some bowlers obtain their slower ball by holding it in the palm of the hand which restricts the flick of wrist and fingers. Perhaps you may discover another and more deceptive method with experimentation.

Of course you practise these in the nets, not in the middle. As a real cricketer, it is your job to understand all the variations, but that does not necessarily mean that you intend to use them.

## THAT EXTRA FAST BOWLER

Most of our discussion has been aimed at bowlers up to fast-medium pace who require subtleties of seam to build an attack. The express fast bowler is an entirely different character who only appears on the cricket scene irregularly.

Many will disagree with me, but my feeling is that if a youngster has real pace, the nurturing of that quality is more important than accuracy, seam or anything else. Cricket history tends to show that truly fast bowlers dominate cricket—particularly a pair of fast bowlers. Lindwall and Miller; Tyson and Statham; Trueman and Statham; Adcock and Heine; Hall and Griffith; Lillee and Thomson—these are the fast bowling combinations since World War II who spearheaded their team's success. Of course most of these men also had accuracy and variety, but their paramount virtue was speed and aggression. They had that extra pace which causes batsmen to consider life and limb as well as simply scoring runs. It was pace more than any other factor that gave them success.

Thus it seems logical that pace is the factor which takes first place. The youngster who is 'quicker than he looks', 'hits the bat hard', or 'gets onto you' should be encouraged to develop a rhythmical approach and bowl fast, even sacrificing a little accuracy for the extra pace if he really has it. After he has consolidated the pace, he can develop the refinements. Too often he is asked to drop his pace to obtain accuracy or swing, and he joins the twenty cents a dozen class.

He will need to learn early to gain lift by digging the ball in short of a length. Certainly the attacking new ball bowlers need to keep the ball up to give it time to move, but the lifting shorter ball is an essential against good players. This controls the batsmen who constantly commit themselves forward looking for drives, as the bowler unsettles such a front-foot player and forces him to adjust his technique. In other words you are bowling away from each batsman's strength. Of course the use of the bouncer is frequently overdone, but there is no doubt that this delivery is an essential part of any fast bowler's equipment. The quickie without a

bouncer seldom really worries a first-class batsman.

One of the major differences between club cricket and first-class cricket is the use of the bouncer. On the harder better-prepared wickets, a pace bowler gains greater and sharper lift. What may have been a long lop on the more 'puddingy' grade wickets becomes a menacing attacking weapon. Most newcomers to State cricket receive a baptism of bumpers. If they visibly wilt, their career becomes an unhappy one as the news of their discomfort travels quickly. Such a player will find the quicks firing away at him all the time, with never a sight of spin until he is able to disprove his reputation of uneasiness against the short-pitched pace. Terry Lee of New South Wales was one of the best club batsmen I have ever seen, yet he never quite made it in Shield cricket because of this very weakness.

So if my advice to a young aspiring pace bowler is to experiment with lift, equally to the young batsman I stress that he must learn to deal with quickish deliveries lifting around the chest and head height. Otherwise his future is very limited in the game.

Let us quickly run over the fundamentals of pace bowling.

1 A rhythmical and smooth approach that aims at you reaching an optimum momentum for delivery. Hops, skips and shuffles in the approach have usually wasted all that precedes them. Most very long runs are wasting energy and effectiveness. Keep the shoulders steady during the approach, then the head remains steady with eyes concentrating on 'the line of attack'.

2 The 'side-on' action, I feel, is the most important. Every youngster should try hard to get into a side delivery, where the back foot is closer to parallel to the bowling crease than at right angles—and where the front shoulder points towards the batsman.

*In my opinion, the greatest of them all, West Indian Wes Hall.*

This requires turning the body from the chest-on position of the approach in the final strides before delivery. Many bowlers develop a diagonal run from a mid-offish position to facilitate this final action.

3  The realisation that both arms are involved in bowling. The left, 'reaching for the sky', will lift the body into delivery. As the arc of the right begins, the left, now tucked into the ribs, will aid body swing. After the ball has gone, the left arm aids balance.

4  A natural follow through behind the ball without falling away from the delivery and so losing body drive. Follow through need never be exaggerated, but equally it should never be cut short forcibly.

5  A knowledge of the individual arc of the arm. I find that many players have little idea where their arm comes over at delivery. Many push the ball down the leg side because the arc of their arms has gone past the vertical towards their heads and they are not aware of it. It is simple to recognise and then correct such an error by asking the bowler to bowl a 'round-armer' with a few witnesses watching. Usually the so-called 'round-armer' is at perfect delivery position. The witnesses are there simply to convince the often doubtful bowler that this is true, and the remedy is to bowl what feels round-arm, but in fact isn't, from here on in.

6  The three-finger grip, even upright rotation of seam, a knowledge of seam and shine effect—these are essential. Each player should be able to recognise which is his natural swing.

7  An enthusiasm to experiment and to try something else used by others, always trying to understand how they are doing it; realising that there are mysteries of bowling yet to be discovered.

8  To realise that an enormous variety is not an essential of fine bowling. A small variety coupled with intelligence, accuracy and determination beats undisciplined use of varieties.

9  To bowl aggressively, trying to bowl players out rather than bore them out. Short of a length bowling to defensive fields is an admission of inadequacy. It is certainly one of the game's greatest curses. If you have the gift of real pace, don't waste it. And most important, be physically fit!

*Jeff Thomson has bowled as fast as any other bowler. Note the side-on slinging action that has created this thunderbolt speed.*

# 9 Wrist-spin

*The basic leg-spin grip. Make a cup with hand and fingers and place half the ball in it. The same grip is used for all variations except the flipper.*

Leg-spinning requires the use of fingers and wrist. The stronger the wrist and fingers, the stronger the flick at point of delivery, and from this comes the extra bounce, spin and zip that all wrist-spinners should be seeking. Bruce Dooland strengthened wrist and fingers by years of squeezing a squash ball; most leg-spinners develop by constant practice. Learn to spin anything cricket-ball shaped, from tennis ball to apple. Spin it to yourself using wrist and fingers, remembering that an orange spun fifty times will always taste better.

Leg-spin of course is a 'right to left' spin created by all fingers moving the ball across the hand from thumb to little finger aided by the wrist, which should add a final flick. Grip the ball as illustrated above. By spinning it from your right hand to your left hand, turning the fingers over the top of the ball from right to left, you have created leg-spin. In your early years you will tend to roll the ball without real zip, but with practice you will hear the snap of spinning fingers. When you are bowling well, you can feel the ball coming off the little finger, something Johnny

Martin and I used to recognise in each other, when fielding; by the additional loop in the air, bounce and bite. Leg-spin is an unnatural motion which makes it rather difficult to control, thus requiring much practice. A budding wrist-spinner must expect to bowl a great deal, preferably a little every day, to master the type.

But though difficult it is interesting, as there is so much variation available. Slight variation of wrist direction when spinning and releasing the ball allows different 'size' leg-breaks through a 90 degree arc. Let me explain.

Spinning the ball from right to left square-on (that is at right angles) to the batsman is theoretically the biggest leg-break. Smaller leg-breaks result as the wrist turns to spin more toward the batsman, until eventually the ball is spun directly toward the batsman over the top of the hand. The latter is an over-spinning top-spinner, a ball that goes straight through despite a wrist action similar to that of the leg-break.

Table tennis players will know that the greater the amount of over-spin, the more the ball drops in the air. Thus the over-spinning top-spinner and the smaller leg-breaks tend to drop quickly and bounce higher from a hard wicket, particularly when bowled against a stiff breeze. The bigger leg-breaks spinning squarer-on with less over-spin will drop less (in fact they usually float on), but frequently drift in toward the right hand batsman before turning away.

It makes sense that the completely square-on leg-spinner should be the largest. On softer wickets, as it bites, it is turning a great deal, but slowly. However, on a hard well-prepared wicket, the square-on spin is unable to grip and the ball skids on straight through, or often skids back from the off with the push of the arm. This makes it an invaluable ball for the leg-spinner as it has the advantage of

*Terry Jenner moves into a correct delivery position with spinning wrist well cocked.*

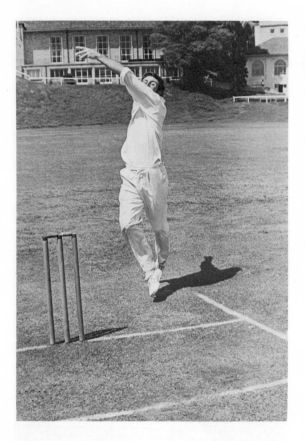 

keeping low so that it can claim leg before wickets or bowl the opponent. This is the back-spinning top-spinner, as frequently the spin has gone past the square-on position and is actually spun backward. Richie Benaud was a master of this delivery and indeed based his attack upon it.

It is a difficult ball to master early, mainly because it is difficult to visualise the concept of spinning backwards in conjunction with the forward movement of your arm. On the other hand, the over-spinning top-spinner usually bounces too high for LBW and is used more for its dropping and bouncing qualities to force lofted shots from an unwary batsman.

Already in the 90 degree arc we can see there is a great deal of variation, from the back-spinning top-spinner through the different sized leg-breaks to the over-spinning top-spinner. Each of these has different flight qualities and each can be fitted into a plan of bowling. But all must be coupled with accuracy to be effective and thus long hours of practice lie ahead.

If we continue this adjustment of the wrist past the over-spinning top-spinner we move into the realm of the googly (or, as it is often called, the wrong'un or bosie). Because the wrist has turned further and the ball leaves the hand over the top of the little finger, the ball now spins from left to right, creating off-spin. Again the amount of spin can be controlled— the closer to the over-spinning top-spinner the less turn obtained, but the greater drop and bounce. The more the wrist is turned, creating 'squarer' off-spin, the more turn plus drift away from the bat occurs.

Early, the leg-spinner should not concern himself with disguising this delivery, simply

*Ian Chappell illustrates the approach, delivery and follow through of the leg-spinner.*

you know how and why something happens and are given a method of practice, the remainder of the learning is up to your perseverance.

Now the method of learning. Start off under-arm over 3 to 4 metres. Hold the ball in the leg-spin grip. Watching your own hand, get the feeling of the 'right to left' wrist-spin, which is leg-spin. Still under-arm, spin the ball out with this spin, making sure that the ball leaves the hand on the side of your arm closest to your leg, that is, 'inside' your arm. This is leg-spin.

Now, with the same grip and type of spin, continue the turn of the wrist until the ball leaves the hand 'outside' your arm. This is the googly. Remember inside your arm must be leg-spin; outside must be a googly. Continue to practise under-arm, watching your hand, so that your mind grasps what movement is required. When you have mastered under-arm, move to round-arm. Now the leg-break comes from 'underneath' the arm; the 'googly' from 'above'. Still watch your wrist and hand, not the result of the delivery. When you are happy with round-arm move to over-arm, still over 3 to 4 metres, and gradually increase the distance of delivery. Now the leg-break is 'outside' the arm, the googly 'inside', although with practice and additional suppleness of the wrist the googly position will come closer to the leg-spinner. If a problem develops, go back to under-arm and start again.

Most boys can learn to bowl a googly within one hour in this way if they understand how it all works. Even for the experienced bowler the method is invaluable—if your leg-spinner or googly is lacking something, you can go back to the under-arm method, analyse your fault and correct it surprisingly quickly. A word of warning! Most boys learning the googly tend to over-bowl it early and often lose the leg-break altogether. If this happens, back you go to the under-arm practice, and all should be well with an hour's thoughtful practice.

gain confidence in bowling it. This often means dropping the left shoulder to gain the leverage to flick the ball over the wrist. Later, however, as the wrist gains suppleness the ball can be flicked over without the exaggerated shoulder movement.

But even if your googly is easily 'picked', don't despair. It still must be played by the batsman and, if bowled accurately, it is a penetrating wicket-taker in its own right, apart from its value as a surprise variation. In fact, many leg-spinners try to develop two googlies: one rather obvious to lull batsmen into false security, the other better disguised. Whatever happens, it must be bowled accurately and should be regarded only as a variation and thus bowled sparingly. Hold it back to keep the batsman looking for it.

How can you learn these deliveries? First you must understand how they work. Once

*The googly (wrong'un or bosie) is flicked over the top of the little finger.*

Thus the wrist-spinner has great variation in spin available to him from the back-spinning top-spinner through an arc almost 180 degrees to the biggest googly. The flipper is another delivery that many great bowlers from Grimmett to Dooland and Pepper to Benaud have used skilfully. It involves a totally different wrist movement to leg-spin, over-spin and googly, however, and is therefore a dubious one to teach youngsters. It is more a post-graduate ball. The ball is held between thumb and fingers and squeezed or flicked out the front of the hand with a similar movement to that performed when 'snapping your fingers'. The ball skids straight through and back into the batsman and comes off the wicket very quickly. It is a great LBW taker.

It is not necessary to master all of these to be a successful leg-spinner but you should understand them and the different flight qualities they possess. Although spin variation is extensive, it is insignificant compared to the thought involved in combining these deliveries into a planned attack, which is the real art of bowling.

## PLANNING YOUR SPIN ATTACK

So you understand the variations of the wrist-spinner from the back-spinning top-spinner through the leg-breaks to the over-spinning top-spinner and into the googlies. You understand that over-spin tends to make the ball drop and bounce, whereas squarer spin tends to aid drift and sometimes skid (the drift always being in the opposite direction to the eventual turn). Furthermore, you have been given a method of learning these deliveries— the under-arm method. If you have the interest to persevere, the mastering of these deliveries is up to you.

But now we come to the combining of these deliveries and developing a planned attack— the real art of bowling.

*First of all, which end should you bowl*

*from?* The majority of wrist-spinners must bowl against the wind. Occasionally a tall strong chap, who pushes the ball through might prefer to bowl with the breeze, but the majority of wrist-spinners look forward to a brisk breeze to bowl against. Most of my comments from here on deal with the flighty leg-spinner rather than the faster type.

Personally, the breeze has always interested me as much as the wicket. A steady head-wind, whether straight down the wicket or from the direction of fine leg or the slips, will aid your spin, drift and drop, enabling you to beat batsmen 'in the air'. The turn from the pitch is usually only finishing off what you have done in the air, as seldom are good players dismissed by a leg-spinner's turn alone. Cross breezes are annoying, but generally speaking I think you are better off in such circumstances to bowl with the breeze from the off. At least that way your drift is aided, even though dropping the ball is not and some leg-spin is blown off the ball. Bowling with a breeze 'up your tail' allows

*The flipper is squeezed out between thumb and index fingers in more of an off-spin flick.*

neither drift, drop nor bounce, and requires a complete rethinking of your plan of attack.

If you spin hard enough you will turn on almost any wicket—concrete, malthoid or top-class turf wickets. You don't need, nor really want, big spin—it is the smaller but fast spin that matters. Usually, the better the batting wicket—and I refer to wickets suited to stroke-making, that is, fast and true—the better it is suited to leg-spinning, *if you have a breeze.* Slow wickets don't suit wrist-spinning, even though they turn a long way; a rain-affected wicket—even a real sticky-dog—is not the leg-spinner's delight.

I have always preferred the Perth ground to bowl on. The wicket is superb. Iron-hard and well grassed, it is fast and bouncy and is a stroke-player's dream. In my opinion, it was Australia's best wicket in my 14 years of first-class cricket. Why did I like to bowl on it? First, because the ball comes off the wicket quickly and bounces, if you have the wrist to create over-spin. Secondly, because of the perennial breeze from the Swan River, 'the Fremantle doctor', which sweeps in during the afternoon. It is strong and blows down wicket, and the bowler who is prepared to spin the ball and throw it in the air is rewarded by tremendous drop and bounce, and (if he gives it a real flick) turn plus nip.

Sydney is my other favourite Australian ground, because of the prevailing north-east or south-east winds. I suppose three-quarters of my overs on the SCG have been from the Randwick end against the friendly nor'easter lazing across the Paddington Hill. Brisbane, too, tends to offer frequent nor'easters, but the wicket, although allowing turn, is ever so slow. The great Melbourne arena I have always disliked for bowling, as wind cannot get past the massive encircling stands, allowing only fitful puffs from any direction; while Adelaide all too frequently offers a cross wind.

The West Indies offered magnificent bowling breezes because the island settings encouraged continuous sea breezes, usually associated with the north-east Trade Winds,

*Intikhab Alam from Pakistan is a successful wristy spinner.*

and nor'easters, of course, come in from over fine leg.

Should you bowl with the wind if the wicket is very slow? I don't think so, as that way you lose everything. Nor do I think you should 'push the ball through' in such circumstances. When attempting to bowl faster for long periods, most flighty bowlers tend to drop short, which is disaster on slow wickets as a good player hits you anywhere at all off the back foot. Frankly, I think you are better on such wickets to bowl more slowly if anything, to ensure keeping the ball up, for you must encourage the batsman to drive in such conditions. If your flight leaves the batsman 'not quite to the ball' the final spin can make driving particularly hazardous on slow wickets.

Clearly, slow wickets don't suit leg-spinners, but unfortunately slow wickets are becoming all too frequent. Fast wickets on

Australian Shield grounds are rare today, while Sydney's grade pitches are usually under-rolled and unhappily slow. 'Unhappily' because slow pitches discourage stroke-play and encourage negative seam or finger-spin bowling.

I don't think I am biased in saying that wrist-spinning is associated with bright cricket, and wickets that suit wrist-spinners are good-cricket wickets. So, for the sake of cricket—and leg-spinners—let's hope to see more hard, well-grassed, faster pitches.

To sum up: when you arrive at the ground check the breeze—it means so much to your bowling. Generally, you pray for a wind from a northerly or southerly direction to bowl against. The sou'easters and nor'westers will aid drift and drop but take off a little spin from your leggie, while the nor'easters and sou'westers are probably your perfect breezes. You don't want an easterly or westerly, but if that's the way it blows, you make the most of them by accepting the in-drift they offer.

## LINE OF ATTACK WITH SPIN

So as flighty leg-spinners we bowl against the breeze that emphasises drift and drop to beat the batsman in the air, remembering that turn usually only finishes off what flight has begun. Of course the wrist and finger flick attempts to create faster spin, not for wide turn but for faster turn, bounce and the effect such spin has on flight. A clearly defined 'loop' in the trajectory of the delivery is characteristic of strong wrist-spin.

Now, what should be our line of attack—that is, what should be the direction in which we are most consistently bowling? There are several answers to this question which I shall discuss, but first I must stress the need for some plan. Certainly this plan might vary for different batsmen, different wickets or different breezes, but there must be a plan. You are not bowling if you are simply wheeling up leg-spinners and googlies vaguely towards 'the other end'.

On good hard wickets, the normal leg-spinner should direct his attack from towards middle to just outside off-stump. Because his basic delivery is the leg-break, this clearly shows that his major strategy is not necessarily to clean bowl the opposing batsman. Young leg-spinners need to learn this early, otherwise they tend to pitch outside the leg-stump in order to spin back toward the stumps. Against a good batsman this is disastrous, and makes it very difficult to set a field.

Imagine, then, we are bowling against a steady north-easterly breeze, the wicket is hard and true, the batsman confident and aggressive. We aim to plug around the off-stump keeping the ball well up to get the batsman on the front foot—we usually want him to come down the wicket at us. The cover field needs to be strong with a short cover, perhaps, to pick up the catch frequently offered when flight leaves the batsman short of his off-drive. We vary our deliveries, perhaps showing a googly early, or skidding a back-spinning top-spinner a little short of a length to tempt the batsman into hitting across the flight off the back foot. But generally we are enticing him down to drive, trying with over-spin to 'drop' the ball, and leave him short of it. We are after the stumping, the edge to keeper or slips, the mis-hit into the off-side field. A major tactic for us is our variation of width, pace and over-spin. The batsman who can drive a ball in line with the off-stump all too frequently forgets that a ball pitched on the same length but 15 to 20 centimetres wider outside the off-stump is further from him. So we let him drive, gradually widen on him, getting a little more drop if possible until, we hope, he is left stranded.

A hint! Watch each batsman's feet when he begins to bat against another bowler. Most players commit themselves either back or forward before the bowler's delivery. That is, the player who wants to get on the back foot because this is his strength begins to do so before you let the ball go, whilst the front-foot driver edges forward. Admittedly this is bad batting technique, but 90 per cent make the error and you, as a bowler, should take advantage of it. If you recognise him as a back-foot player, throw the ball up further; if a front-foot player, make it difficult for him to drive. In other words, bowl what he doesn't want.

A second line of attack is middle and leg. For this you need great accuracy—certainly in consistency of length—and usually the top-spinner is a major part of your offence. Richie Benaud frequently attacked here with Alan Davidson stationed at leg-gully. His back-spinning top-spinner was a beauty—the best I have seen—and often made up half of the deliveries. So well directed was his attack that he bowled without an out-fieldsman on the leg-side; he concentrated on complete accuracy coupled with drop and bounce.

Thirdly, some leg-spinners bowl wide of the off-stump to a powerful off-side field. In particular, this occurs where batting conditions are so perfect that the bowler is trying to close up the game. I cannot accept such a method as it is completely negative and basically aims at 'boring' the batsman out. When a leg-spinner adopts such an approach we might as well pack up and give the game away as, of all bowlers, he must always think aggressively and be prepared to 'buy' wickets if necessary.

Finally, whatever our line, we must be able to keep near the plan. Without it we are unable to 'work' on the batsman; without it the captain cannot place a reasonably economical field, and the batsman can sit on us scoring comfortably without taking any risks. Thus we must practise to bowl tight; to be able to introduce variations of spin, pace, flight, bounce and width without great loss of accuracy. That is not easy and takes much practice, concentration and perseverance— maybe years and years of it.

## HOW FAST?

How fast should a leg-spinner bowl?

Every delivery must be made with body and shoulder fully behind it, plus a powerful wrist- and finger-spin. As long as you are doing this, you cannot bowl too slowly. For with the body swing and follow through you will nip off the wicket, whilst the swiftly spinning ball will do some strange things lofted in the various breezes. The slow-flighted bowler has the advantage of drift and drop—he has a well-defined looping trajectory.

But I must stress the original proviso: the need for full body and shoulder drive. If you are simply rolling the ball up into the air without body behind the delivery, you will lack subtleties of flight and any nip off the wicket. You may worry many batsmen with your high trajectory, but never the better players.

So there is your answer. *Remember that everyone is different, and that there is a natural speed for each bowler. As long as your body and shoulder are working fully in delivery, there is no need to speed up.*

So many youngsters, trying to bowl faster than is natural for them, lose all accuracy, particularly in length. They bowl an occasional unplayable ball but are usually so erratic that they become uneconomical for the captain.

Usually the taller leg-spinners of first-class cricket have been quicker. The Bill O'Reillys, the Richie Benauds, the Cecil Peppers and now the Kerry O'Keefes have pushed the ball through much faster than smaller men of the fraternity such as Arthur Mailey, Colin McCool, Clarrie Grimmett and Johnny Martin. *But this is not to say that one group was right and the other wrong.*

Their particular method suited the big men as they pushed the ball down and through at the batsman, relying on bounce and zip and accuracy. On turning wickets, they become most difficult; on hard and fast batting wickets, they sometimes had difficulty turning the ball. On the other hand, the smaller men of flight usually spun on any wicket and relished the hard, fast batting

wickets, but frequently were a little too slow on real turners such as rain-affected wickets. So it is simply a matter of different types. Determine what is most natural for you as an individual, and then work hard on that type.

The plan of attack will differ for each type. Basically, the slower bowler tries to bring batsmen forward, whereas the quicker type tries to push him back. Where the slower bowler should be prepared to 'buy a wicket' when the batsmen are on top, the quicker one needs to bowl with nagging accuracy on such an occasion to force them into error.

But whatever the type, whatever the plan, there is a great deal of thought and hard work involved. To gain the necessary wrist flick, variations of spin, flight and bounce, plus accuracy, requires years of dedicated practice. It also requires a philosophical understanding that there will be hidings on occasions, things will go wrong, and only hard work and patient concentration will overcome these problems. In the long run, the returns are worthwhile. The first time your googly leaves the opposing batsman bewildered; when your top-spinner nips off and traps the back-foot player in front; when extra over-spin drops the ball and leaves him stranded up the wicket—these things will bring a great sense of achievement to balance the 0–100, and towering sixers over mid-on.

Any player who has bowled wrist-spinners over a number of years would go through it all again, given the opportunity.

I have stressed the need to understand and master variations in spin, in drop, in drift and in bounce; and the need to plan an attack, perhaps varying it for different batsmen with different weaknesses. We have discussed line of attack and bowling speed for wrist-spinners.

One word of warning, however. All these variations and strategies must be built upon a basis of accuracy. Length and direction must be consistent. And most important, young bowlers should learn not to 'try too hard'. Many of us have learnt this by bitter experience over long years; I hope you can save time here. By not 'trying too hard' I mean not trying to bowl out your opponent every ball; not trying to bowl eight different varieties each over. Nine times out of ten you are a more effective wicket-taker if you simply get out there and bowl, working to your line of attack, introducing the occasional variation and trying to drop on the spot. By all means search for individual weaknesses and 'work' on the batsmen, but bowl tight, particularly concentrating on the accuracy of your basic delivery, the leg-spinner. Your googlies, top-spinners and so on are variations; the leg-spinner is your bread and butter, and if it is not taking wickets you are usually bowling badly. Against tail-enders especially, bowlers tend to become greedy and expect wickets every ball, going through the entire box of tricks. Usually these subtleties are wasted on the tail, the bowling pattern is interrupted and valuable runs are wasted. So bowl tight.

It is a fact of life that if you bowl badly early, you are unlikely to bowl for long; and if you don't bowl for long, your chances of accuracy become less. So young leg-spinners must work hard on achieving respectable opening overs whilst warming up.

First, get your hands and fingers warm before you bowl and loosen up before your first over arrives. Then in your first over, think more of bowling a maiden than taking eight wickets. Start on a line well outside off-stump and wait until you settle down before moving in to your normal line. Whatever happens do not allow yourself to stray to the leg-side. Also bowl too full rather than too short.

Remember that if your first couple of overs are accurate and economical, you can gain confidence and settle down. On the other hand, early looseness and a hiding destroys your confidence and, worse still, your captain's confidence in you. And without his confidence your bowling opportunities will be limited.

To gain accuracy requires much practice and too many bowlers practise unin-

telligently. They simply get into the nets, run up mechanically and bowl until concentration, strength or interest runs out. Here are a few suggestions to increase the effectiveness of your bowling practices.

You are aiming to develop certain skills when you bowl at practice.
1  Accuracy is one I have stressed.
2  Variation of all types as described.
3  Concentration—the most important factor of all.
4  Spotting individual strengths and weaknesses.
5  Increasing stamina.
6  Pure enjoyment.

*Kerry O'Keefe is a quicker, flatter type. With less turn, he often depends on accuracy alone.*

*This series of shots shows the moment every spinner plans for. Tony Greig goes down the wicket, is deceived by flight and beaten. Rod Marsh finishes off the exercise to the delight of Redpath and the disgust of Greig.*

Consider the following activities that can be introduced to attain these by breaking up long bowling sessions into sections.

1 For accuracy, set aside an over here and there where you nominate to yourself the length and direction you wish for each ball before bowling. You may be surprised by your early lack of success, and pleased by your rapid improvement. Of course accuracy will carry over into your general bowling practices.

2 For variation skills, spend more time with a friend away from the nets and over 8 to 10 metres, and then devote five to ten minutes to these in the nets each practice. It may take months, or years, to master a delivery to the extent where you will bowl it in a match.

3 Concentration—set aside six or eight balls here and there, bowl to a field you have placed mentally, keeping an honest record of your figures for that over. Repeat at intervals. Then go back to simply bowling to dismiss your opposing batsman.

4 The spotting of strengths and weaknesses

goes on as you bowl, as you field, as you have a breather—for the real cricketer this activity never ends.

5 & 6 Stamina will come from long 'spells' (and, by the way, what a misnomer for such hard work) in matches and the nets, but to gain the enjoyment is a matter of sensible variation of practice. By breaking up your practice in this way at your own discretion, you will find you can bowl longer, without losing concentration, and in so doing can acquire more readily all the contemplated skills.

Finally a word to the coach and/or interested parent. Encourage a youngster who shows interest in, and aptitude for, wrist-spinning. There will be many times when he considers turning to seam bowling or finger-spinning or to specialist batting, for his youth in the game is often very disappointing as he tries to master the most difficult of all bowling skills. This is particularly so at the school-leaving stage, when he is no longer spoon-fed for practice and must find his own time and make a few sacrifices.

# 10 Finger-spin

Because of the mechanical structure of wrist and shoulder, the leg-spinner, as we have discussed, can utilise great leverage to spin the ball. This certainly enables him to turn more than any other bowler, provided, of course, he does use all fingers and wrist to full advantage rather than 'rolling' the ball out. As well, we have noted the great variety of spin, drift, drop and bounce available to the wrist-spinner. But such spin requires a relatively unnatural and difficult action. Thus the major disadvantage tends to be the problem of accuracy. The overall result is that wrist-spinners tend to be wicket-takers rather than run-restricters; they need to have a mentally aggressive orientation towards attack. Of course, the best leg-spinners are also accurate, but for the developing youngster we can forgive some looseness in his quest for penetration.

The finger-spinner frequently needs a different mental approach. Leverage is physically restricted which means that turn is limited on good wickets. But accuracy should present few problems to this bowler, because the action is a natural and simple one. On the good wickets, he may be forced to rely on persistent accuracy, coupled with variations we shall discuss shortly, in order to 'bore' batsmen out. Certainly in such conditions, he tries to be a run-restricter, and it is fair to say that the bowler who cannot bowl off-spinners very tightly should not bowl them at all. If he consistently bowls this bad ball per over, he is a nightmare to the captain, for the batsman can safely 'sit' on such a bowler. This means he plays the majority of the over, scores from the loose deliveries, and is placed under no pressure either to survive or to score. At this stage the bowler is not a wicket-taking danger, nor is he restricting the score.

On damp or dusty wickets, the finger-spinner comes into his own. In these conditions, the wrist-spinner may be too slow, spin too far or lack the pinpoint accuracy of the finger-spinner, who can increase pace with little loss of length and direction.

So each type has its place in an attack. In damper conditions, the wrist-spinner has limited opportunities, and the finger-spinner dominates the game; on the hard sun-baked wickets, wrist-spin is often needed in order to extract turn. But neither type is superior to the other; they are simply different, and each prospers in suitable conditions. The young spinner needs to learn which suits him best both temperamentally and physically.

## VARIATIONS OF SPIN AND FLIGHT

The index finger is the crux of finger-spin. Imagine there is a clock in front of you with the big hand on twelve o'clock. Put your index finger on the big hand and quickly turn it to three o'clock. This is the clockwise off-spin movement. Although the major spinning finger is the index finger, second finger and wrist should equally aid the final flick.

To gain additional clockwise leverage, separate index and second fingers as far as possible. You will now feel the index finger pulling back in the off-spin direction. Some bowlers eventually tuck the index finger beneath the ball to increase leverage, but youngsters should take care just how soon and how far they separate these important spinning fingers.

Check the orthodox grip. Hold the ball in your left hand with the seam facing across your body.

Place the right index finger on the seam at twelve o'clock. Now place the second finger at three o'clock and screw the ball in tight between those two fingers and the bend, 'non-working' third finger.

*Bishen Bedi, the great Indian left arm finger-spinner, stretches his muscles whilst warming up before practice.*

At this stage, the ball should be firm in there without the thumb touching the ball. Whatever happens don't allow the thumb to hold beneath the ball; instead rest it up beside the index finger.

To learn what is basically a simple action, many youngsters respond best to a throwing action, which allows the elbow to aid the wrist and fingers. In pairs, they can throw off-spinners to one another with any kind of ball over 5 to 8 metres. Once they perfect this, they can iron out the throw to a legitimate bowling action but still recall the wrist and finger flick that created the off-spin. Gradually the distance can be increased.

Using a tennis ball for this is a rewarding exercise. The tennis ball will *drift away* considerably before it spins back (just as *leg-spin drifts in to a batsman before turning away*). In this way, the off-spinner's invaluable out-drift ability is well illustrated.

To bowl the out-curve, the off-spinner must accentuate his side-on delivery position in the same way as an out-swing bowler. He also gets in close to the stumps if bowling over the wicket. He does not seam the ball, however (see the chapter on seam and pace to explain this), but spins the off-spinner with a slightly lower arm and uses the true out-swing follow through with the arm and body. Clearly he will obtain the most effective out-drift with a breeze to help it, such as the north-easter coming from fine leg. In such conditions in Sydney, Fred Titmus bent his off-spinners prodigiously.

Generally, however, the bowler should try to deliver the ball with as high an arm position as possible. This will aid not only spin but

*Finger-spin*

*Another angle showing Bedi just before delivery.*

*Bedi moves into copy-book delivery position.*

bounce, which, as I have said before in wrist-spin discussions, is as valuable as turn. Jim Laker's action was perfection in this regard.

Over-spin, with its qualities of drop and bounce, can also be introduced by the adjustment of hand and wrist. Now the index finger spins over the top of the ball more towards the batsman. Thrown into the air against the breeze, this delivery will drop quickly and bounce higher; it is an invaluable variation on the harder batting wickets. Lance Gibbs bowled it superbly, but his West India-rubber joints allowed him to adjust to the required action more easily than most. You will need to practise the delivery for some time.

What we are discussing is in fact a similar proposition to the wrist-spinning adjustments but in the opposite direction. The index finger goes over the top towards the batsman for over-spin, gradually moving in a clearer clock-wise movement across the batsman to increase turn and drift. Experiment with these finger adjustments, and once again try to develop a real flick instead of simply cutting the ball.

The introduction of a normal out-swinger is common. This delivery (explained in the chapter on seam and pace) is quite similar in action but requires slight adjustments of grip and wrist movement. The best method is to hold the ball with exactly the same grip as mentioned on page 80. The seam should be pointing across your body, from off to leg. Now, keeping your grip the same, rotate the ball around until the seam points towards first slip with the index finger along the seam. To bowl your off-spinners from this grip, you twist from twelve to three towards fine leg as usual. To bowl the arm ball, however, and so create out-drift, your index finger drives straight on towards first slip. The seam is released with even upright rotation towards first slip and out-swing results.

In practice, the left arm finger-spinner (that is, the leg-spinner) seems to utilise this ball more frequently than the right arm version. It is often referred to as the 'arm-ball' which comes back in to the right hand batsman as variation to the away moving leg-spin. It may be bowled at normal pace, slower or faster, but most left armers push it through faster, hoping to seam back through the batsman's defence before he detects the variation. But the slower arm ball is also valuable, and too often neglected. Because it is slower, it has more time to drift further; and because it is more flighted, it tempts the batsman to come down the wicket to drive. Big drift into your feet can make this footwork hazardous.

Of course variations of feet positions along the crease will vary angles of delivery. When bowling over the wicket, the angle of the out-drifter is accentuated if delivered from close to the stumps, whilst the off-spinner appears to turn more from a position wider on the crease. The finger-spinner particularly should utilise both 'over' and 'around' the wicket positions. As turn increases, he may move around the wicket to decrease his angle, and force batsmen to play at him.

We have already discussed the variations of spin, drift and drop; the bowler can also use slight changes of pace. So despite his physical limitations of wrist leverage, the finger-spinner has a great variety at his disposal. With control of his stock ball, he can develop a very testing attack. It is essential that right from the start he clearly understand how his methods will differ for good batting wickets and 'turners'.

## THE LINE OF ATTACK AND PLAN OF ATTACK

Like the leg-spinner, the wrist-spinner will alter his line for different batsmen and different conditions. With these alterations, field placements too will change. But once again it is essential that some plan of attack is employed, so that the bowler does not bowl thoughtlessly and mechanically. In discussing plans, I assume good control, for, as I have stated, a player who cannot control finger-spinners immaculately should not bowl them at all.

## Finger-spin

On good wickets with little turn, the bowler must concentrate his attack on one side of the wicket only, as he cannot expect to defend both sides with nine fieldsmen. Many once bowled at the leg-stump with a powerful leg-side field, but this is now restricted by legislation that limits the on-side fieldsmen to five.

Others concentrate on an accurate line just outside off-stump with a six-three field (that is, six on the off-side and three on the leg). With accuracy they are able to bowl away from each batsman's strength. For instance for the strong front-foot driver who tends to 'itch' forward, they speed up a little just short of a length as the stock ball; for the back-foot player, more flighted and fuller deliveries become the stock. Once again watch each batsman's feet to determine his individual preference.

But this is only your stock ball upon which to base an attack; to forget all else but such accuracy in order to contain batsmen is negative and defensive. For your own enjoyment and that of others, I hope you choose to be a positive aggressive bowler.

The variations to go with your stock ball are clear cut. The more flighted over-spinner to bring the batsman down the wicket; the widening of deliveries on the batsman as described in leg-spinning; the out-drifter; the variations of feet positions on the crease; the arm ball; changes of pace—all these may be introduced. But once again the bowler who regularly tries to 'bowl the lot' each over will suffer inaccuracy, and will have no stock ball upon which to base an attack. When batsmen are playing well on good batting wickets, you must be patient. Be prepared to bowl tight, to tie the batsman down, so that when the slower ball or drifter is bowled, he may be forced into taking a risk he might normally forego. Frequently the batsman will have his eye on your thinly manned on-side field and will be looking to sweep, pull or loft any misdirected deliveries. A short off-spinner of normal pace can be pulled through the leg-field even when pitched well outside off-stump, whilst

*John Emburey is one of the world's top present day spinners. Note the drive of his right arm across his body and the position of his spinning fingers.*

anything in line with leg-stump is open to punishment. Thus both length and line need good control.

If you have control of an out-drifter, don't use it early, but tie the batsman down outside off-stump. Then as he becomes restless produce an out-drifter on line of leg-stump. Over-eager, he may commit himself for the sweep or on-drive, only to find himself in trouble as the ball drifts to off-stump. Similarly when a batsman is looking for the pull, you might let him have a shorter ball—but a little faster and wider of off-stump.

On the other hand, if you feel yourself getting on top—or if a wicket is needed fast—and you are oozing confidence, be prepared to 'mix them up'. Tony Lock adapted magnificently to Australian conditions once he settled in Perth. He was able to restrict you with his accuracy, but when conditions suited he introduced a great variety that included different run-ups, all the variations discussed, as well as descriptive and colourful adjectives.

If you are on the attack, crowd the new batsman or the less confident one. If there is little turn but drift, a short cover and gully slip will pressurise the batsman. As the ball begins to turn, however, mishits will tend to fly more on the on-side than off. Shortish mid-ons, or even silly mid-on, short legs and even leg-gullies are now the pressure positions. You must recognise the major wicket-taking fielding positions for your bowling as conditions change.

If the batsmen begin to settle in and attack, withdraw the field and fall back to a more restrictive plan. But usually one of the pair shows less confidence or competence, and he should be attacked and pressurised where possible. Push the fieldsmen up around him, then defend to his partner. Don't too easily give in to total defence.

When the ball begins to turn sharply on a dusty or wet wicket, the off-spinner is in his element. Attacking fieldsmen can crowd in on the on-side with covering fieldsmen at mid-on and mid-wicket. In fact he needs more than five on the leg-side as big off-spin and bounce

*Fred Titmus was one of the most successful English off-spinners under Australian conditions. He had a superb arm ball.*

*The best off-spinner I have faced—Lance Gibbs.
He was a master of flight. Note the widely spread
index and middle fingers of his grip.*

*John Gleeson was a finger-spinner with a difference. He developed something unorthodox and made a successful Test career of it.*

makes attacking off-side shots almost impossible. But the rules now limit fieldsmen to five on the on-side, and the bowler must work hard to force batsmen to play at him. This may necessitate his going around the wicket to reduce angles.

In these conditions, the off-spinner's ability to push the ball through without loss of accuracy makes survival difficult for all but the most nimble footed, and usually there is little need for much variation. Plug away with your stock off-spin using what the wicket has to offer, and results will come. Whatever happens *do not bowl short on these wickets; keep the ball up and force the batsman to play forward. It is better to err on the full side.*

## IVERSON-GLEESON METHODS

Years ago the googly was an unorthodox and mysterious delivery. It has of course become a straightforward delivery because players understand how it is bowled and meet it frequently.

The same acceptance will come for the Iverson-Gleeson type of delivery, which still confounds many batsmen. When we examine and understand these deliveries, they too are straightforward and simple to detect.

Jack Iverson apparently conceived this spin type when flicking a table tennis ball in his fingers. His gigantic hands easily adapted this to a cricket ball.

Let's examine the method. The ball is held between the thumb and bent middle finger, and spin is imparted by the flicking and straightening of that finger. The remainder of the fingers do not participate, which means that the middle finger is solely responsible for spin. Clearly your fingers must be strong, and preferably your hand large.

To allow the middle finger to flick the ball in an anti-clockwise direction (leg-spin), the bent middle finger must be outside the ball. Thus for a leg-break the hand cuts *outside the ball*—the normal off-break position.

For the off-spin, the hand must turn inside the ball to allow the middle finger to flick the

ball with a clockwise spin. Such a hand position is that of an orthodox leg-spinner, yet for Iverson and Gleeson it creates off-spin.

So the confusion of this type is simply that it is a reversal of the orthodox. When you understand this, there is no mystery involved.

John Gleeson very intelligently adapted himself to this method after years of wicket-keeping. He added an orthodox off-spinner—a logical variation—and a seamer. But the critics who discuss his 'googly' etc. are simply revealing their ignorance of his methods, for this 'googly' is his Iverson-type off-spin. In fact John bowls three types of spinners only—the Iverson off-break, the Iverson leg-break and an orthodox off-spinner.

There are two lessons for young bowlers here:

1 If batsmen or critics want to imagine an immense variety or a particular mystery ball, never contradict them. Do not add to the myth either, but remain quiet and let it grow. I remember years ago, when opponents claimed they picked my googly because I grunted when bowling it. They were wrong, as I grunted most of the time—but why should I dispel such a rumour. In time it spread to my advantage.

2 Be prepared to experiment. As I said earlier, there are different deliveries yet to be discovered, and the rewards for the innovators such as Bosanquet, Iverson and Gleeson are great. So experiment with grips and ideas.

Eventually I see the Iverson method being best employed by an orthodox off-spinner. Instead of a basic Iverson attack with occasional orthodox off-spin, there is a great future for an accurate off-spinner who produces a difficult to detect leg-spinner every now and then. I visualise such a bowler causing great concern amongst batsmen, and young off-spinners might be well rewarded for experimentation in this field.

*Here Boycott fails to pick Gleeson's leg-break, plays along the wrong line and is caught in slips by Stackpole.*

# SECTION III FIELDING

# 11 Skills in Fielding

I have no doubt that fielding is the most vital part of cricket. 'Catches win matches' is an old cry, whilst the difficulties created for batsmen by a lively, aggressive, run-hungry fielding team are known to most of us. Yet the need to practise and broaden knowledge of fielding skills and tactics is all too often overlooked.

If a cricketer cannot enjoy fielding when young, he might as well retire at once, for he will spend more time fielding than batting and bowling combined. And there is a great deal to enjoy in fielding.

First, there is the awareness of being part of a drilled, intelligent, aggressive group whose total energy is centred on the dismissal of batsmen. Secondly, there is the simple matter of being closer to the game in progress, and thereby being able to involve yourself more fully in its development and to scrutinise the individual players. Thirdly, there is the enjoyment of throwing yourself whole-heartedly into a physical and mental activity to the very best of your ability. Fielding can be a hardship for a hard-working bowler on occasions, but for the remainder, without these pressures and responsibilities, there is no reason why it should not be sheer joy.

In choosing any team, selectors must carefully assess fielding capabilities. They must have an effective fielding unit, and to build this I don't believe they can afford to choose specialist batsmen who are not good fieldsmen. Indeed, in first-class cricket these days, a batting specialist must make himself a brilliant fieldsman somewhere or he is poor value. If mobility or throwing arm is lacking, he must make himself into an outstanding close-to-the-wicket field. If he lacks the reflexes or temperament for in-fielding, he must develop his pace, hands and throwing to become a competent out-fieldsman. There is a place for most players somewhere if they are prepared to work at it, but if they cannot or will not find a place, they must accept a limited potential in the game.

There is some excuse for a bowler to lapse in the field. It can be difficult to retain energy and concentration in both bowling and fielding after twenty or thirty overs, but he must try, for a team can ill-afford more than one weakness. The bowler who develops his fielding often gains preference over another, whilst it is a wonderful team bonus to have pace men such as Fred Trueman or Graham Mackenzie who were great fieldsmen in their own right. So my advice to any young ambitious bowler is to try and develop a specialist skill in fielding. In modern cricket, a bowler plus slips field *is* an all-rounder.

The time will come when your arm and mobility have gone and your close-catching is

*Bob Taylor pops one up at Lords and a flying Kim Hughes takes a good catch.*

*The greatest slips catcher Australia has produced since World War II—Bobby Simpson. Here he takes another slips catch off Alan Davidson. Remember he was fielding here at first slip, so notice the ground he has covered.*

deteriorating and unreliable. Despite your other strengths, you are now a liability to your team and it is time to move gracefully out of competitive cricket. The young player without the drive or interest to develop his fielding should not be there making a burden of himself in the first place. With determination and energy, it is amazing how he can improve himself if he goes about it intelligently.

How can you develop your fielding?

1 Learn the skills and methods of fielding. Involve yourself in discussions of fielding as much as any other part of the game; don't make the mistake of regarding it as a minor department of the game.

2 Practise the skills hard and *get yourself fit*. A day in the field is hard work—as hard as a rugby game—and you need physical fitness to retain your enthusiasm and energy to the end. How much easier the game bcomes when you are fully fit! You can face up to being night-watchman, or giving a final bowling effort. You must finish the day with plenty in reserve, accepting the fact that tiredness is never an excuse for lack of performance. Whether you obtain this fitness from cricket practice, from running or from a gymnasium is immaterial, but do yourself a favour and get fit.

3 You must learn to retain your concentration in the field. To help you, I suggest the following. Whilst fielding, try to gauge the strengths and weaknesses of each opponent. How can you as an individual help to counter his strengths? What would you bowl to him? What field would you set? What is your captain's plan? What will he want from your bowlers? What will he want of you? And so on.

Now I'm not suggesting that you continually approach your captain to pass on these ideas; nor do I suggest you follow your plan rather than follow your captain. This is solely a means of involving yourself

deeply in the development of the game, of remaining alert and of constantly thinking about what is required on the field, instead of drifting off mentally to the races or the beach—often an attractive daydream when the temperatures soar into the 90s.

You should never force your captain to clap and wave to move you. It may be essential to his plan to move you 10 metres inconspicuously. You should be watching, alert and concentrating; preferably foreseeing his manoeuvre. For instance, in a partnership involving a stronger and a weaker batsman, you must be prepared to give a single to the stronger player early in the over if the captain so desires, and to restrict his singles later in the over. To make it easy for the baymen on such occasions is pure bad cricket. You must read the game yourself and expect tactics and counter-tactics, rather leave it all to the captain alone.

4 Clearly then, the more you know about the game as a whole, the better you are likely to field. Thus another aid to fielding is an all-round education in the game; the 'real' cricketer as I have defined him previously is usually the best fieldsman.

If all of your eleven were to follow these principles, captaincy would be a far simpler task. Of course the pressures and problems of a captain increase as you go up the scale of cricket, but in many ways the job becomes easier. Frankly I found the captaincy of New South Wales a simpler task than a club side, for the very reason that more players at State level know the game.

Finally to the coach: Teach fielding as you teach every other phase of cricket. With constant drill and supervision, with enthusiasm and practice, there is no reason why young players with reasonable ability cannot field like a Test team. They have an age advantage related to eyesight, reflexes and mobility; they are at their physical peak. No matter how much an older player retains his enthusiasm, the youngster always has this advantage. He lacks the experience and know-how, of course, but good coaching can broaden these. *Of all the cricket skills, fielding can be more easily developed by the coach than any other—and it is the most important.*

## GROUND FIELDING

When a batsman meets a team that moves in briskly with the bowler, always moves quickly to the ball, throws accurately and smartly—always sprinting and oozing confidence—and shows a miserly reluctance to surrender easy runs, he knows he is in for a hard day. He can feel the atmosphere and the determination that aims to make things as tough for him as possible. The bowlers are also aware of it and lift their efforts accordingly.

Thus, all fieldsmen—other than those in close-catching positions—move in towards the batsman as the bowler begins his approach, speeding up, leaning forward and getting up on their toes as the ball approaches the batsman.

*Each fieldsman wants the ball to come to him; he wants to participate as often as possible; to do as much as he can in the field rather than as little.*

To give away singles at the wrong time should be regarded as a disgrace. If batsmen hit short singles to you, you should regard it as a direct insult not to be repeated. These become personal challenges to you as an individual fieldsman. In the out-field of course you can seldom restrict singles, but you can cut down on twos and threes by getting in to the ball as quickly as possible. This often means running in a straight line to the estimated point of interception rather than circling around the boundary. So sprint hard everywhere, be prepared to get your body in the way, to dive—to do anything to cut off runs. This requires an aggressive attitude and complete confidence in your hands, which comes with practice.

With careful observation and growing

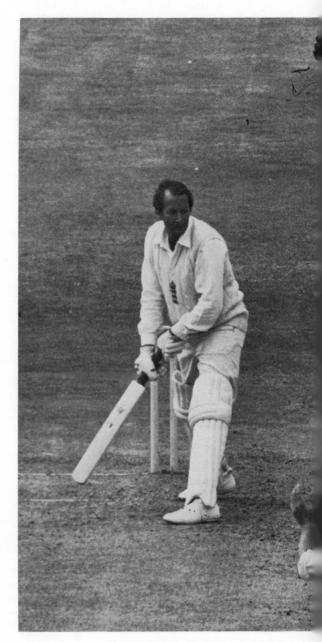

*Greg Chappell lunges left to pick up D'Oliveira off Mallett.*

*Fielding should be practised more than any other part of the game. Here Bill Lawry leads some basic close catching practice. Fortunately fielding practice techniques have developed more than any other part of the game over the last ten years.*

experience you come to position yourself more quickly. By watching the ball onto the bat, you become aware of differing angles of deflection for each batsman. You begin to move towards the ball immediately (it appears almost prior to contact) and you get there with plenty of time. The great players—the Harveys, the Sobers, the Davidsons—always seem unhurried. The greatest catches often look easy because of this; many more spectacular catches have come from slow lead-up work.

When you do make an error, whether catching or ground-fielding—and everyone does—recover quickly. Don't stand there cursing your ill-fortune, stupidity or incompetence, move quickly to compensate for it. Your team-mates realise you are not trying to make errors and that you regret them, they require no demonstration. So do your best to make up for your mistake at once. Many a run-out has been obtained from a quick recovery after an initial fielding error.

The day when you can look around and have confidence in all your team-mates in the field signals the achievement of an ultimate position which few experience. You know that each player will give all, energetically and intelligently. You know that as a break in play approaches, they will lift their efforts for a breakthrough rather than allow their efforts to tail off in anticipation of a rest. This participation is the most thrilling experience in cricket, just as it is its most thrilling spectacle.

Once again a coach can create this if talent is reasonable. Sloppy fielding indicates sloppy coaching and/or sloppy captaincy, for practice, instruction and drill, drill, drill can achieve any levels.

Normal practices are too often based on fieldsmen scattered 30 metres from the bat, gathering and returning to a wicket-keeper as the ball comes to them. This requires variation. Here are some suggestions:

**Number the group**   The hitter calls a number and that player fields the ball wherever it goes, and returns to the bat. As they warm up, call the same number four, five or six times consecutively. Push the player to sprint, to bend, to get his throw away smartly, to keep at it. The smaller the group, the more work for each individual.

Perhaps you can call a number adding 'run-out' or 'no run-out'. The player should react differently to each circumstance.

*For the run-out* a fieldsman must take risks to *move into the ball* as quickly as possible, picking it up clearly and getting the throw away at once. In this case risk extra runs rather than play safety first. Now you will sprint low and fast *with eye on the ball* towards the interception point and, as you near this, turn side-on with front shoulder pointing at the ball. This requires an adjustment of your stride to pick up the ball on the most convenient half volley, and usually involves a rhythmical side-on run.

Constant drill makes it second nature and enables you to consider your next move, the throw, whilst approaching the ball.

The throw is got away at once with speed, with no wind up or balancing steps. From the in-field such a throw will come from below the shoulder, whilst from the out-field the over-the-top baseball throw is preferable. The former puts greater strain on elbow and shoulder.

When a run-out is on, you cannot consider the hands of keeper, fieldsmen or bowler; your throw must be your most powerful unless the batsman is so far out of his ground that you can afford to steady yourself. Mostly your throw should be to the waiting wicket-keeper, bowler or fieldsman, rather than at the stumps themselves, although occasionally the time comes when a direct throw is the only possible means of dismissal. But either way, you throw hard and this involves risk.

The team as a whole must realise this and back up all such throws. If possible a fieldsman replaces the bowler at the stumps—behind them rather than in front or beside them—whilst other fieldsmen back up this receiver to support him. Back up in depth—20 or 30 metres back if possible, rather than 4 or 5 metres behind for here you are unsighted and, following a deflection, quite helpless. Every player should try to participate somehow in a run-out attempt, living up to the ideal of trying to find the maximum to do rather than the minimum.

*For 'no run-out'* risks are unnecessary. Now the player can adopt the more defensive and reliable fielding positions with both legs, or knee plus thigh, safely behind the ball. The ball is returned at brisk medium-pace with accuracy and preferably baseball style.

1 This conserves the throwing arm. Many youngsters get carried away with the strength and power of their arm and over-use it. This is particularly dangerous in cricket where we are so often forced to throw 'cold'. If you have a good arm, look after it. Once it 'goes', it does not come back—*and it can happen to you.*

2 It also involves the concept of hiding your arm from the batsman. An experienced batsman quickly tries to assess the fielding and throwing capacity of each fieldsman as he bats. If you use your arm only when necessary, you may surprise a batsman and pick up a run-out for your team. Even when you know a player has a good arm, his sensible saving of it can surprise you as many of us have found to our disgust.

3 This avoids the possibility of unnecessary overthrows.

4 It saves the hands and energy of your wicket-keeper.

This discussion also brings to mind the need for fieldsmen to look after their bowlers. When the ball goes back to the bowler, it must do so on the full. If you cannot be certain of getting it there on the full, give it to someone else who can, but whatever happens don't force the bowler to bend, stretch or jump unnecessarily. His job is difficult enough already, so try to help him. In my schoolboy teams, an error in this regard cost at least twenty press-ups.

When a team fails to dry carefully a wet ball, wiping the seam to keep water out, or when a team carelessly returns the ball to keeper or bowler it indicates a laziness, incompetence or lack of know-how. An experienced onlooker immediately notices these failures in out-cricket which indicate poor team work and poor cricket education. So do even the apparently small things with care.

Place a set of stumps in the ground between two groups of three players each 30 metres from the stumps. The game begins with a player throwing at the stumps, the opposing players run in onto that throw, gather it on the run and get their throw away. This continues with each side scoring a point for a direct hit and, if you wish, the loss of a point for misfielding.

*The techniques of ground fielding and throwing must be learnt and drilled.*

*A warning: With this exercise and any other involving hard throwing make sure the players warm up before they begin.*

Split the team into two balanced groups, omitting the wicket-keeper. Put in a stump in centre-field with the keeper in position. One group is scattered in the off-side fielding positions from backward point to mid-off in single saving positions. The coach now hits out twenty ground balls one after the other around all fieldsmen. For each one, he awards points from nought to three depending on the speed of movement to the ball, the pick-up and the throw. The non-participating group counts the hits, totals the points scored, and backs up the wicket-keeper. After twenty hits, the groups change.

**'Forcing-back'** The team is split into two groups. Mark out a rough rectangular field about 50 to 60 metres long and, for six-a-side, about 30 metres wide. Groups defend opposite ends of this field and score a point by throwing the ball across the opposition goal line. The ball must be thrown along the ground, with a penalty being awarded against any throw which is in the air at all.

Players can move quickly around the field to cut off the opposition throws and return them on the run. With practice, the players will dive, sprint and bend to make cut offs. It is a magnificent game for all ground fielding skills as well as team spirit.

**'Soccer-cricket'** This is another great game in its own right, which entails all the ground fielding skills but particularly encourages fast-moving interception. A rectangular field similar to the one above is roughly marked and 3 metre goals are also marked with bats, boots and stumps at each end.

The game is played as soccer, except that a cricket ball is bowled under-arm instead of a soccer ball kicked. Players do not run with the ball in their possession—although they may dribble it—but pass it to one another, with the eventual aim of bowling it through the goal. It is fast-moving exercise, great fun and wonderful ground fielding drill.

**Continuous cricket** Your group is divided into two teams. The fielding team scatters around the field only in front of the wicket with one bowler. The bowler stands about ten metres from the batsman, delivering the ball under-arm at three stumps. When the batsman hits the ball he must run, and scores by running around a stump located ten metres away square of the wicket.

If he is bowled or caught out, when fieldsmen gather the ball they return it to the bowler who bowls at the stumps whether the batsman has completed his run or not. Swap the bowlers around. When one team is out, the other bats.

**Paddox** Similar to the above, but played along 20 metres with two wickets. The ball is bowled or thrown from either end whether the batsman is ready or not. There are several bowlers at each end. A batsman can be bowled, caught or run-out and scores a run when he and his partner cross.

There are many other games which you can develop and incorporate into practices. You can devise them yourself. The games will help to make fielding sheer good fun—but at the same time dedication and hard work are needed. Keep it moving fast, insist on high standards and full effort, introduce variation and encourage humour to make the whole affair thoroughly enjoyable.

## CLOSE CATCHING, PARTICULARLY SLIPS CATCHING

In modern cricket, most players at some stage must occupy a close catching position. They need to consider the skills of the slips specialist who is so vital to team performance. In fact this player becomes almost as significant as the wicket-keeper, and in many ways needs to develop similar techniques.

*First,* hand technique must be correct. This involves hand positions where fingers never point towards the ball. When the ball flies low, fingers point down; above solar plexus height, fingers point up. Bending the elbows

*To develop your close catching, correct hand technique must be learnt. Two hands work together to keep the eyes near the ball; fingers never point at the ball.*

allows you to position down-pointing fingers higher than normal, but the stomach-high catch still remains the most difficult, for a snap decision must be made whether to catch in a down-finger or up-finger position. Bob Simpson overcame this problem in this situation by frequently hugging the ball into his body, which is effective but rather severe on the ribs.

Try to give with the ball, to cushion it in and so avoid snatching or being 'hard handed'. There is seldom a slap when a ball is taken by a gifted wicket-keeper, as the ball is 'absorbed' gently into his hands. Throughout the tour of the West Indies in 1965 whilst fielding slip next to Wally Grout, I seldom if ever *heard the ball* enter his gloves.

So work on hand technique whenever you are practising slips catching. Of course there will be occasions when speed of events will not allow perfection, but generally the slips fieldsman who is technically sound is the most consistent.

*Secondly,* you must really believe that every ball is coming to you. Again I must mention Wally Grout to illustrate this, when in Brisbane he took the greatest wicket-keeping catch I have seen. Queensland had taken a battering from New South Wales, spending the whole day in the field with temperatures in the 90s. In the last over of the day, a Tom Vivers' off-spinner jumped unexpectedly off a length to an in-form Graham Thomas already over the century. Because he was seeing the ball so well, Graham managed to get a glove to the ball and the deflection flew quickly straight over his head.

Grout, crouched behind the stumps, straightened and leapt up arms full-stretched.

*The close catching fieldsman adopts the same hand positions (or 'glove work') as the wicket-keeper.*

*Bob Cowper has reversed his hands to the upward-pointing finger position as he sets himself for the catch above stomach height.*

He took the ball so easily in two hands that the majority of spectators failed to understand that they had witnessed a miraculous catch. In the morning it would have been a great catch—at five to six it was incredible. Grout's concentration had not lapsed; he still expected every ball to come to him.

A slips fieldsman like a wicket-keeper should not normally anticipate. You will be tempted to do so, occasionally fall to the temptation and even make a great catch created by anticipation; but for every great catch made, you will miss three that would have been easy by staying in position. So stand your ground, imagining that every ball is yours. This requires prolonged concentration, which can make slips fielding most exhausting. To retain concentration, you must relax between deliveries.

I encourage some talking in slips ('the social positions') before the bowler commences his approach, but then concentration must be complete. I must stress again that with observation of deflections over a period of time, you begin to move towards a snick more quickly. This often appears to be anticipation by the onlooker, but it is instead

*Another catch to Allan Border off the bowling of Terry Alderman. Border proved himself to be both Australia's top batsman and most reliable slips catcher in 1981. Note his hands' and eyes' position for a catch which came sharply at a difficult height.*

103

an instantaneous reaction nurtured by experience. The player moves into position quickly and gets *two* hands onto the ball with apparent ease, whilst a less gifted or less experienced player may be forced to dive. I repeat that the greatest catches are not always the most spectacular, and often the most thrilling looking catch has resulted from early slowness.

At first slip you may watch the ball all the way through the approach, delivery and in flight. You can do this because it requires no change of head and eye position. But from second slip and wider—particularly gully—to follow the ball all the way risks a momentary unsighting. Therefore from here your eyes concentrate on the edge of the bat alone.

It is preferable not to crouch with feet wide apart. This is likely to restrict your mobility. When moving to the ball, try to get both hands to it, as this will bring your eyes closer to the line. I preferred to fall to a low catch for this reason rather than stretching. The most difficult low catch for a right hander is at his left toe, and kicking your legs out of the way and falling with two hands is your best method here. Of course there will be occasions when the only way to get to the ball is with a one-handed dive.

*Thirdly,* positioning is important. So that all players can go for any snick without worry of interference or collision, it is essential that they are well spaced and well angled. Most youngsters stand too close together and in so doing often leave a halfway ball to the other through misunderstanding. Just as bad, they formulate local rules such as 'You catch on your right hand'.

If you think you have any chance at all, go for the snick—dive if necessary. This means you must be more than a double arm's length apart and angled so that second slip is a metre ahead of first, third a metre ahead of second and so on. Slips never field in a straight line. Now each fieldsman can go for anything with complete safety.

*Fourthly,* in fielding to slow bowlers you must decide whether you are essentially up for

*In the out-field, the hands still work together. Ian Chappell has his hands held high so that he will never lose sight of the ball. The fingers are extended and not pointing at the ball.*

the front-foot snick or back for the back-foot snick. It is seldom possible to be reliable for both at the same time, and standing in no man's land leaves you reliable for neither.

For example, if you are positioned up, wide and close to the bat of a leg-spinner looking for an edge or shoulder as the batsman lunges forward, you cannot really be expected to catch a snick from a back-foot slash at a short ball. If you do take such a catch, it should be regarded as a bonus, and the bowler must recognise this. The captain, bowler and slip must make a decision whether they are primarily looking for back- or front-foot chances, and accept the results philo-sophically.

*Concentration in the slips—Ian Chappell, Greg Chappell, Doug Walters and Ashley Mallett. Note that Greg Chappell has his little fingers overlapped to help lock the hands.*

There are many practices that can be used to develop slips catching.

1 Hitting sharp catches to a semi-circle of fieldsmen who return the ball to the bat is a basic one—the smaller the group, the more frequent the catches for each individual. Add interest by punishing a dropped catch by press-ups or wind-sprints, or bring the offending player to the centre to catch the next six himself. You can make a game of it by allowing the catchers twenty runs for a catch taken, and penalising them one wicket for a catch dropped. In this way, play a Test match.

2 Stand a boy 10 to 15 metres away as a pitcher. The remainder form a slips cordon. You take the bat to edge and guide the thrown ball into the cordon. (I suggest you stand in a side-on position, with bent back knee, so that you can sway from the line of erratic throws.) Again you can make some game or competition of it, or simply push the youngster to the 'gully end' as he drops a catch.

3 Divide your group into pairs about 8 metres apart. Now they throw the ball under-arm as hard as they wish but below the knee, backwards and forwards to one another. The longer they can take this the better, but you may choose to declare the first to drop ten catches as the loser. Run a team knock-out competition.

4 For youngsters, an exercise that brings great amusement and skill is to stand in the middle of a circle and flick a series of

throws around amongst them. Through the legs, behind the back, slower ones, faster ones—mix them up, keep it snappy. It is good for their reflexes and concentration.

5  The use of a roller, slips 'cradle' or slips 'net' is straightforward if you have these aids. Concentrate on short sharp catches, however, rather than the long distance very hard ones.

Close catching is difficult. There is seldom an easy catch, because of the problem of prolonged concentration. I am a great believer in allowing a slip out for a run every now and then to relax him. A run around the boundary or a sprint in the covers is a relief after some hours in slips. As well, if a player puts a few down and appears to be losing confidence, think seriously of relieving him temporarily. The catches seem to chase you in slips when you are having a bad day, and if confidence goes you have no chance of taking them.

The captain needs to treat the situation with diplomacy of course. He must not dramatise the affair into an expulsion to the salt-mines. He unobtrusively replaces the slip, with confidence that he will appreciate the temporary move. And temporary it must be, for as the thrown horse rider must soon try to get back in the saddle, so if the fieldsman has ability in slips he must be encouraged back in there again.

## CATCHING GENERALLY

For the ball high in the air, reach the hands towards eye level with fingers spread to form a cup. See both the ball and the hands all the way, so that there is no moment when you lose sight of the ball—as you must do when hands are at stomach height.

Again try to avoid fingers pointing at the ball and allow the hands to give with the impact—the 'cushion effect'. Quite clearly, the most important point is to position your body correctly beneath the falling ball. Don't get too far away from it. Probably the baseball technique for catching out-field hits

is soundest. Like a slips catch, hand position is reversed above and below chest height. Fingers never point at the ball, and if we examine the up-pointing finger technique for higher catches, it becomes clear that ball and hands are always in sight and that eyes, hands and ball are constantly 'in line'.

For a youngster, the forming of a cup with the hands beneath the ball is a useful start. For the very young, get them to catch a balloon rather than a ball, since this emphasises the need to avoid snatching. Once again always try to use two hands, and retain your aggressive, adventurous approach for catching. If there is a chance of a catch, go for it. Take a risk of losing runs in order to score the catch, rather than playing safety first.

You can develop games and practices to drill these skills, adapting ideas from the ground fielding methods suggested earlier.

Again I must stress the necessity of varying the practices mentioned to keep them fast moving, energetic and plain good fun. A well-organised fielding practice involves the demonstration, discussion and practice of a skill, followed by the drilling of several fielding skills, followed by a skill game.

## FIELD PLACEMENTS

All fieldsmen should accept as one of their duties the understanding and memorisation of field placements for each of their bowlers under different conditions. Certainly the bowler and captain must control the placements, but it is not good enough for fieldsmen to leave it all to them and helplessly await directions. Try to anticipate the fielding requirements for the team as a whole and yourself in particular, recognising the

**Top right**  *A correctly positioned slips cordon. The players are well apart, each a metre ahead of the finer slip. This way each slip can fall or dive without danger of collision.*

**Right**  *Jeff Thomson's slip cordon to Mike Denness.*

catching positions, defensive positions etc. All too often, when a new bowler enters the attack, young fieldsmen make no effort to move towards their probable positions, but simply stand there waiting to be moved.

At this stage with young players, it is worthwhile checking their knowledge of names given to fielding positions. Gather them in a group around a pitch, and one by one ask them to occupy a named position. Keep this up snappily until all positions have been occupied several times. A mistake costs five press-ups to jog the memory.

Once they know the terminology it is time to recognise the qualities required in these positions.

1 Quick reflexes, good hands and lots of concentration begin to equip a slips or close catching fieldsman, but with this must go an evenness of temperament, a coolness and lack of flamboyance.

2 A good turn of speed, agility, aggression, good hands and an accurate, speedy throwing arm are requirements for an in-fieldsman (point, cover-point, cover, extra-cover, mid-off, mid-on, mid-wicket, square-leg).

3 A strong, fast runner with a strong throwing arm will succeed in the out-field (fine leg, third man, deep square-leg, long-on etc.).

Which of these qualities are yours? If you fill the bill for 1, 2 and 3 you are one of the fortunate all-round fieldsmen like Alan Davidson. If you can see no position to suit your abilities, you need to work hard on skills to master some positions.

Now let's examine some orthodox fields set for different types of bowlers. Where do you see your skills being used for each bowler?

It is absolutely impossible and pointless to

treat fielding positions such as these other than in the most basic way. Fielding positions are not decided according to the bowler alone, for different fields should be set for individual batsmen and for varying conditions.

To position a series of textbook fields for different bowlers is not captaincy. The captain must use his imagination to create the field necessary for the particular circumstance—there is no such thing as an orthodox field placement. Here are some factors that must be considered in placing any field.

1 *We should always attack batsmen when we can* and put pressure on them. When players settle in, we may gradually relieve pressure, moving the field back into more defensive positions to save runs. But with a change of batsmen—or conditions, or bowlers, or some other circumstances such as closeness to an adjournment in play—we

*Ian Chappell sets an attacking field to David Colley. Nine of the eleven fieldsmen are in the picture. Always attack when possible, particularly against a new batsman.*

*Close set fields coupled with accurate bowling put pressure on batsmen. Be prepared to crowd the batsman when you get on top, as Underwood crowds Davies in this picture.*

must try to attack again. Often this entails attacking one batsman and defending the other, thereby doing as much bowling at the weaker player as possible. Knowledgeable fieldsmen now can really help their captain.

2 One player may be strong on the back foot; another on the front. One may be strong with square shots; the other straight. One may be essentially an off-side player; the other leg-side. Therefore our field placement must be flexible enough to attack or defend accordingly—generally (but not always) working on the principle of playing away from each man's strengths.

3 Be aware of the differences in running between wickets of batsmen. The faster man needs to slow himself down to his slower partner, but many of them do not and with an alert field plus slight field adjustments, run-outs can be forced. Similarly as a batsman tires, his running can be used to advantage. The tiring batsman naturally slows down whilst his more energetic—and perhaps nervous—partner may fail to appreciate this. They are liable to run-outs, if the field as a whole is awake to the circumstances.

4 Most players are nervous when they begin an innings—some very nervous indeed. The longer the fielding team can restrict such players from scoring, the less chance they have of settling down. In the same way, a player can be pressurised when he is on 49 or on 99 (or even on 87 these days), for the magical numbers can sometimes lead him into indiscretion.

Experience will make you aware of innumerable occasions when you must adjust your basic field. My advice to any young captain or bowler is that if an aggressive scheme for dismissing a batsman flashes into your head, have a go at it at once. *Don't delay, don't frighten yourself into safety first. Be confident, be adventurous and try your tactic.*
For these reasons, it is difficult to state just what an orthodox field is for a particular type of bowling.

Each individual must work hard on the development of his fielding ability and knowledge, every team must work harder at fielding than any other activity. If the team is a fine fielding unit it will be successful; if the fielding is sloppy or incompetent *nothing* can compensate for that weakness.